D0938102

ART DECO

MetroBooks

Metro Books
122 Fifth Ave.
New York, NY 10011

This edition published by Metrobooks by arrangement with Parragon Publishing

Copyright © Parragon 2001

M 10 9 8 7 6 5 4 3 2 1

The right of Iain Zaczek to be identified as the author of this
work has been asserted in accordance with Section 77 of the
Copyright, Designs and Patents Act of 1988.

The right of Mike O'Mahoney to be identified as the author of
the introduction to this book has been asserted in accordance with
Section 77 of the Copyright, Designs and Patents Act of 1988.

ISBN 1-4114-0148-4

Printed and bound in Indonesia

ART DECO

IAIN ZACZEK

Introduction by Mike O'Mahoney

MetroBooks

CONTENTS

CONTENTS

INTRODUCTION

Art Deco belongs to a world of luxury and decadence, the Golden Age of the 1920s and 1930s. The very term conjures up a multitude of romantic images: huge ocean liners gliding effortlessly across moonlit seas; the sounds of clinking cocktail glasses and a raucous jazz band emanating from a sumptuously decorated ballroom; a Busby Berkeley spectacular showing in one of the newly built movie theaters ornamented with Egyptian-revival columns and Aztec motifs; or the gleaming skyscrapers of the Manhattan skyline and sun-soaked white stucco villas of Miami Beach. Art Deco is characterized by a range of exquisitely designed art and craft products. These include the paintings of Tamara de Lempicka (1898–1980) and Georgia O'Keeffe (1887–1986), ceramics by Clarice Cliff (1899–1972), fashion designs by Paul Poiret (1879–1944) and Coco Chanel (1883–1971), jewelry by Louis Cartier (1819–1904), metalwork by Jean Puiforcat (1897–1945), and posters by Cassandre (1901–68). Even mundane objects, like vacuum cleaners and Bakelite radios, were given the Deco treatment, adorned with smooth surfaces and sleek lines reminiscent of the most modern automobile.

Despite this utopian emphasis on luxury, Art Deco emerged in an era of economic slumps and depressions, social strife, hunger marches, and the political battle between Communism and Fascism. It was against this troubled and traumatic backdrop that Art Deco forged its own identity. Art Deco, essentially, was an eclectic style; its artists and designers plundered a diversity of historical sources. Simultaneously, however, it emphasized modernity, employing the latest industrial materials and techniques. Indeed it was this fusion of history and modernity that gave Art Deco its unique character. Ultimately, this world of exuberance, vitality, and beauty was a world of fantasy, a world as escapist as any of the Hollywood musicals of the same era. Its legacy, however, is one of great beauty, craft, and imagination.

The term Art Deco, deriving from the French, Arts Décoratifs, is somewhat misleading as it is a label that was applied retrospectively. Indeed it is but one of many terms subsequently coined to describe the decorative arts of the 1920s and 1930s. Other popular terms include; "The Jazz Style", "Jazz Modern", "Style Poiret"and "Style Chanel" (after the fashion designers), "Paris 25", "Style 1925", and "La Mode 1925". These latter three labels reveal the significance of the year 1925 for the emergence of the Deco style. In particular they indicate the importance of a major international exhibition, titled L'Exposition Internationale des Arts Décoratifs et Industriels Modernes, staged that year in Paris. Originally planned for 1915 but postponed because of the First World War, it was a celebration of modernity. At the same time, however, it recognized a need to reconcile two seemingly opposing spheres of activity, the industrial and the artistic. Accordingly, many contributors to the exhibition not only embraced modern materials but also a modern approach to artistic production. In essence, this meant artists no longer ignoring the everyday needs of society and forging a separate identity, but rather applying their aesthetic skills to all aspects of design, ranging from architecture and interior decoration to fashion and jewelry. As Walter Gropius (1883–1969), the founder of the Bauhaus school, had earlier claimed, "There is no difference in kind between the artist and the craftsman. The artist is merely an inspired craftsman." This attitude was manifested in the diversity of the national pavilions which constituted the focus of the 1925 exhibition. The shift in emphasis from the Fine Arts to Arts Décoratifs acted as a catalyst for many artists and designers and effectively launched Art Deco on the world stage.

While the 1925 Paris exhibition is identified as the key event in the development of Art Deco, features of the style had begun to appear in embryonic form over the previous quarter of a century. It originally emerged as a direct response to Art Nouveau, the style that reigned supreme at the turn of the century and dominated the 1900 *Exposition Universelle,* also staged in Paris. Drawing much of its inspiration from the natural world, Art Nouveau adopted sinuous, curvilinear forms, and undulating shapes, reminiscent of plant stems, petals, and filaments. While Art Nouveau practitioners did not reject Modern materials and techniques, they were frequently disguised so that decoration and aesthetic beauty dominated any sense of function. Art Nouveau has frequently been interpreted as a continuation of the policies earlier established in Great Britain by William Morris (1834–96) and the Arts and Crafts Movement. Morris and his colleagues, reacting to what they perceived as the low quality of industrially produced goods exhibited at London's Great Exhibition, of 1851, promoted a return to craftsmanship and extolled the virtues of handmade products. By the early twentieth century, however, these values were increasingly being challenged. In an era of technological revolution that witnessed the development of the motor car, major expansions in telegraphy and telephony, and the first manned flight, the machine was seen as more relevant to a world of modernity and progress than the decorative details of Art Nouveau.

A major precursor in this shift away from Art Nouveau and towards a new, modern style was the Scottish architect and designer Charles Rennie Mackintosh (1868–1928). Together with his Glasgow-based colleagues, Mackintosh initially maintained a significant degree of Art Nouveau ornamentation in his work. However, he increasingly pared down these decorative elements in favor of a starkly elegant and geometrically inspired aesthetic. In 1900, Mackintosh was invited to exhibit several of his designs in Vienna. Here his works struck a chord with a number of young

Viennese artists and designers who were themselves gradually discarding the ornate decoration of Art Nouveau for a more geometrically based style. Chief amongst these was the architect-designer Josef Hoffmann (1870–1956).

Like Mackintosh, Hoffmann's first works were strongly affiliated with the Art Nouveau style. He believed in top-quality design and manufacture and the use of carefully selected, and frequently expensive, materials. Moreover, he promoted the idea that the artist-designer should participate in every aspect of the production of a work, down to the merest detail. In 1903 he founded a company known as the Wiener Werkstätte (Vienna Workshops) where he and his colleagues oversaw every aspect of the design of each project they worked on. Significantly, Hoffmann did not reject the machine as a means of production. On the contrary he claimed that any refusal to engage with modern materials and techniques could only constitute an anachronistic "swimming against the current". Hoffmann's best known architectural work, the Palais Stoclet in Brussels (1908), suggests the ways in which he was moving away from the decorative emphasis of Art Nouveau and towards a more holistically designed, geometrically inspired, architectural style. Hoffmann's Palais Stoclet stands half way between Art Nouveau and the newly emergent style that was to become Art Deco. While extraneous detail is reduced in favor of a seemingly more functional approach—the external façade of the building relates directly to the uses of its internal spaces—Hoffmann never loses sight of the aesthetic qualities of the materials used. The resulting building is simultaneously functional and exquisitely luxurious.

By the early 1920s, in the wake of the First World War, the notion of functionalism had taken on a new and more vital significance. The destruction and devastation caused by modern technological weapons during the conflict demanded a reassessment of the utopian potential of the machine. Yet for some, like the architect-designer Le Corbusier (1887–1965), the machine still offered a way forwards, a means of rebuilding the social infrastructure of a post-war nation. Le Corbusier, originally a follower of the Cubist movement, promoted a new stylistic vocabulary based upon the order, clarity, and standardization he valued in modern industrial processes. Nonetheless, his new aesthetic fused both the past and the present. In the journal *L'Esprit Nouveau*, Le Corbusier compared the classical temples of Ancient Greece and Rome to modern machines—automobiles, ocean liners, and aeroplanes. In particular, he claimed that functional design carried an intrinsic beauty all of its own, distinct from the prevalent desire to hide the functional elements of an object under a façade of extraneous decoration. Despite Le Corbusier's emphasis on standardization and functionality, however, many of the buildings and objects that he designed as prototypes were actually manufactured from relatively expensive materials and were frequently handcrafted.

The functionalism promoted by Le Corbusier also found roots in Germany at the Bauhaus school. Here decoration was specifically rejected in favor of a greater emphasis on simple, "honest" forms. Whilst Bauhaus designs were always sparse and less inviting than the exuberant Art Deco, its functionalism nonetheless influenced the development of the Art Deco style. However, the notion of aesthetic beauty was never abandoned in favor of utility. The two ideas were fused, giving rise to a new term to underpin Art Deco philosophy: "beautility".

When Art Deco artists and designers looked to the past for inspiration, they looked far and wide. Numerous sources have been recorded in the development of an Art Deco aesthetic. These include African tribal art, Ancient Egyptian culture, Assyrian art, Central American art and architecture, and the eastern exoticism of

Sergei Diaghilev's (1872–1929) Ballets Russes. Interests in African tribal art in early twentieth-century Europe were inextricably linked with the recent period of colonial expansion. Examples of tribal art were frequently gathered on colonial expeditions and displayed in specially designated sections in the major international exhibitions of the day. In Paris, the foundation in 1878 of the Ethnographical Museum, later known as the Trocadero, was highly influential in introducing African art to European audiences. Many modern painters, including André Derain (1880–1954) and Pablo Picasso (1881–1973), responded to this presentation by borrowing stylistic features from tribal culture and introducing them into their own essentially western art forms. The influence of African tribal art on the development of the Deco style is perhaps most evident in the design of pots and vases, many of which use motifs deriving from works displayed in the Trocadero or, later, at the Great Colonial Exhibition of 1931. Problematically, the Deco style was also associated with emerging stereotypical representations of African-American performers, particularly in popular entertainment and jazz idioms. The most notorious example of this comes in the costumes, sets, and posters designed for the 1925 production of the Revue Nègre, staged at the Théâtre des Champs-Elysées and featuring the singer-dancer Josephine Baker.

In addition to its fascination with African tribal culture, Art Deco also embraced stylistic motifs from Ancient Egyptian art and architecture. In 1922, at a key moment in the emergence of the Deco style, the world was captivated by the news of the discovery of the tomb of Tutankhamun by the archaeologist Howard Carter. This fascination acquired an extra level of mystery and intrigue with the sudden death of Carter's sponsor, Lord Carnarvon, and the spread of apocryphal stories concerning a possible curse. More importantly, the huge treasure-trove found in the tomb remained news for nearly a decade as objects were gradually brought into daylight and revealed to an eagerly awaiting audience. The Art Deco Egyptian Revival, sometimes irreverently referred to as "Tutmania" or the "Nile Style", perhaps manifested itself most strikingly in the field of architecture. The 1920s saw the continuing growth of the movie industry and the building of many new cinemas throughout the United States and Europe. These palaces for the masses were sumptuously decorated to further the impression of escape into a fantasy world. Egyptian motifs were frequently incorporated into both the exterior and interior designs. Tragically, many of these buildings have now been demolished or refurbished. Others, such as the Carlton Cinema in Essex Road, London, can still be seen in all their glory.

Factories were also designed in the Egyptian revival style. One of the best-known examples remaining today is the Hoover Factory in West London. The Egyptian Revival style can also be found in a multitude of other Art Deco objects. For example, jewelry and clocks designed by Louis Cartier, frequently used turquoise, a material much associated with the age of the pharaohs. Other decorative objects, including table lamps and figurines, were decorated with motifs such as the palm frond or scarab beetle inspired by decorations from the vast collections of Egyptian and Assyrian art that could be seen in museums.

The impact of Central American art upon Art Deco has been given less emphasis than other historical sources; yet an awareness of Aztec and Mayan cultures influenced many Art Deco designers to a considerable degree. Aztec stepped pyramids, for example, provided the inspiration for any number of small objects including clocks and radios. On a larger scale, the stepped-pyramid design offered a solution to the problems of many New York architects. In the period of the great skyscrapers, Manhattan zoning laws required that buildings narrowed as they ascended to allow sufficient light to reach ground level. Here, the stepped pyramid provided a suitable model. The addition of Aztec and Mayan decorative elements, both internally and externally, helped to promote an air of luxuriant historicism around essentially modern buildings.

In 1909, the arrival in Paris of Sergei Diaghilev's Ballets Russes triggered a huge interest in eastern cultures—this was subsequently to impact upon the whole Art Deco aesthetic. The Parisian fashion world, in particular, quickly absorbed the exoticism of Leon Bakst's costume and stage sets for performances of Rimsky-Korsakov's (1844–1908) *Schéhérazade* and Stravinsky's (1882–1971) *The Firebird*. Ballets Russes performances continued to influence European art and design throughout the subsequent two decades. Perhaps its biggest impact upon Art Deco can be seen in the fashion designs of Paul Poiret and Erté (the pseudonym for Romain de Tirtoff (1892–1990)), the ceramics of Clarice Cliff, and the work of the French glassmaker René Lalique (1860–1945).

Today, over half a century since its heyday, the legacy of Art Deco continues to be seen and felt all around us. In architecture, some of the greatest monuments to the utopianism of the period still have the ability to capture the collective imagination. For example, the great skyscrapers of New York, including the Chrysler Building, the Empire State Building, and the Rockefeller Center, remain dominant features on the Manhattan skyline both through their size and their reputation. In Miami Beach, Florida, the exclusive villas and hotels of the Art Deco era continue to exude the sense of luxury and glamor with which they were originally associated. In London, even a train ride on the underground passes through Art Deco stations, such as Arnos Grove, while a trip to the zoo introduces us to the wonderfully eccentric, Deco-inspired animal enclosure designed by Berthold Lubetkin, a veritable Miami Beach Hotel for penguins.

In painting too, the legacy of the Deco period remains very much in the public eye. The canvases of Tamara de Lempicka, such as her famous *Self-Portrait in a Car* (1925), make regular appearances in exhibitions, book publications, and poster reproductions and continue to influence our vision of the excitement and adventure of the Roaring Twenties. Furthermore, her brightly colored and sharply delineated portraits of famous people and sensuous representations of women have helped to redefine our understanding of the nature of art production during the inter-war years. Similarly, the work of Georgia O'Keeffe, whether focusing upon the dramatic and exhilarating cityscapes of New York, or the seemingly more mundane forms and surfaces of flowers and vegetables, reveals a fascination with careful design, decoration, and exquisite finish, all true characteristics of the Deco style.

The public nature of much Art Deco painting, especially the production of murals, has also helped to ensure its preservation. One sad exception, however, is that of the glass mural depicting the *History of Navigation*, designed by Jean Dupas (1882–1964) and installed in the Grand Salon of the famous ocean liner the SS *Normandie*. In the era before transatlantic flights were commonplace, the *Normandie* represented the epitome of modern high-speed travel. To enhance its international reputation, the French government entrusted the decoration of the liner's interior to the finest Art Deco artists and designers of the day including the silversmith Jean Puiforcat, the ceramicist Jean Luce, the furniture designer Jean Dunand, and the glassmaker René Lalique. Dupas' mural, along with the work of these leading artists and designers transformed the *Normandie* into a floating palace dedicated to the Art Deco aesthetic. Tragically, however, the liner suffered an ignominious end when it sank in New York harbor in 1942.

The *Normandie* continues to capture the public imagination, however, both through the Art Deco objects which were saved from the wreckage and the numerous poster designs advertising its services. Most notable amongst these latter are a series designed by Cassandre. Although ostensibly ephemeral items, these and other

Art Deco posters by artists such as Cassandre, Edward McKnight Kauffer (1890–1954), and Jean Dupas have been preserved and are now much sought after by both museums and private collectors. Indeed Deco objects continue to make their presence felt in the modern world. Art Deco graphics, furniture, metalwork, ceramics, glass, textiles, fashion, and jewelry still attract significant audiences at exhibitions whilst the names of many of the main practitioners, including Georges Lepape (1881–1947), Süe et Mare, Ferdinand Preiss (1882–1943), Emile-Jacques Ruhlmann (1879–1953), and Ettore Bugatti can still be found on the auction lists. Reproductions of classic Art Deco items, such as Clarice Cliff ceramics and René Lalique glassware, can also be found in major department stores whilst many movie theaters and theaters whose original Deco interiors have long since disappeared are being given a facelift in a notably Deco-inspired style.

Yet the greatest evidence of the enduring fascination with Art Deco resides in the influence the movement has had upon contemporary artists, designers, and architects. A classic example of Art Deco revivalism can be seen in the MI6 Headquarters Building in London. With its slick, decorative, and highly detailed façade it rises from the River Thames like the fantasy stage set to a 1930s Hollywood spectacular. This paean to the decadence and romance of the Deco era provides evidence of the endurance and popularity of the style that was Art Deco.

MIKE O'MAHONEY

CHRYSLER BUILDING, NEW YORK (1928-30)
William van Alen (1882–1954)

Courtesy of the Architectural Association/Joe Kerr

This is perhaps the most famous of all Art Deco buildings. The designs were initially commissioned by William Reynolds, a land developer, and then passed to the new owner of the property, Walter P. Chrysler. As a car tycoon, Chrysler was anxious that the building should reflect the glory of the industry that had brought him his fortune. At the corners of the 40th floor, at the base of the building's central section, the architect was instructed to include a frieze of car wheels and four sculptures of hubcaps with wings. Similarly, the apex of the structure featured the chevrons that formed part of the Chrysler company logo. It is said that the owner gave orders that a set of tools should be placed beneath the Chrysler's spire, but removed them on the very day that the Empire State Building stole its thunder to become the world's tallest structure.

The Chrysler Building displays a number of classic Art Deco features. It conforms to a basic, stepped pattern, narrowing as it reaches its peak. It also gives the impression of representing a huge sunburst, the most popular of all Art Deco motifs. This effect is achieved by the triangular dormer windows, which are featured in the top seven floors.

PALAIS STOCLET, BRUSSELS (1905–11)
Josef Hoffmann (1870–1956)
Courtesy of the Architectural Association / Peter Willis

The Palais Stoclet is generally recognized as one of the formative influences on Art Deco design. In 1905, Josef Hoffmann was invited to build a new residence for the wealthy Belgian financier, Adolphe Stoclet. His brief was to design a splendid mansion that would also serve as a showcase for Stoclet's extensive art collection. The result was a genuine surprise. While Brussels was one of the bastions of the flowing, curvilinear Art Nouveau style, Hoffmann's palace was angularity itself. It brought together an assemblage of jutting, rectilinear forms, which were asymmetrical but extremely well balanced. The highlight of the exterior was a remarkable stepped tower, with four hieratic statues at the apex. For the interior, Hoffmann enlisted the services of colleagues from the Vienna Secession. Carl Czeschka (1878–1960) produced a range of stained glass, while Gustav Klimt added a stunning series of mosaics, entitled *The Stoclet Frieze* (1909–11).

The stark linearity is often cited in support of the argument that Art Deco evolved as a direct reaction against the excesses of Art Nouveau. This is far from certain. Instead, Hoffmann is more likely to have drawn inspiration from the work of Charles Rennie Mackintosh (1868–1928), another figure who bridged the two very different styles.

EMPIRE STATE BUILDING, NEW YORK (1930–32)
Shreve, Lamb & Harmon

Courtesy of the Architectural Association / Dennis Wheatley

Although it is probably the most famous of New York's skyscrapers, the Empire State Building was created under very difficult conditions. The Wall Street Crash took place in October 1929, just one month after a five-man consortium, headed by John Jacob Raskob of General Motors, had given the architects permission to proceed. The deal still went ahead, but the construction schedule had to be drastically altered. Under the watchful eye of Shreve, Lamb, & Harmon, work began in March 1930, on the site of the old Waldorf-Astoria Hotel. The structure took shape, at the phenomenal rate of four-and-a-half floors per week—the entire, 102-story building was completed in a record-breaking 410 days. Site managers even managed to keep their costs below the $50 million that had been budgeted.

The Empire State Building has the basic, stepped outline that is common to most Art Deco skyscrapers but, for obvious reasons of economy, its interior decoration is comparatively restrained. The most striking feature is the entrance lobby, which is lined with Rose Famosa marble and contains a monumental brass relief. This relief has a stylized depiction of the building, inscribed with the words "the eighth wonder of the world."

SOUTH BEACH, MIAMI, FLORIDA (1930s)
Various Architects

Courtesy of Arcaid/Natalie Tepper

It might easily be imagined that the best place to see American Art Deco would be in New York, but in fact the finest selection can be found at the other side of the country, in Miami. Here, the Deco District provides a living record of this vibrant era. In keeping with its warm, southern climate, the Art Deco motifs have a tropical flavor. There are murals of flamingoes, giant portholes, and many of the buildings are painted in bright, candy-stripe colors. Characteristic examples include the Cardozo Hotel on Ocean Drive, the Miami Beach Post Office, and the Beach Patrol headquarters.

Awareness of these treasures led to the creation of the US's very first conservation schemes. In 1976, Barbara Captiman set up the MDPL (Miami Design Preservation League), to halt the growing threat of demolition of the Deco District. The first meeting attracted just six members, but Captiman persisted with her crusade and, in 1979, the League succeeded in having 900 buildings in the South Beach area placed on the National Register of Historic Places. At the time, this was the only collection of 20th-century US buildings to be protected in this way. The MDPL is still in operation, and its headquarters offers an information service to tourists about the district.

THE BERKELEY SHORE HOTEL, MIAMI (1940)
Albert Anis

Courtesy of the Architectural Association / Rene Davids

By a curious irony, Miami owes much of its rich Art Deco heritage to a spate of bad weather. In the early 1920s, the city was in the middle of a phenomenal property boom. New buildings were rising week by week and, in 1925 alone, almost 500 new hotels and apartment blocks were added to the Miami Beach skyline. Then, a year later, disaster struck. One of the worst hurricanes in local history devastated the coastline, killing more than a hundred people and sweeping away much of the shoreside habitation. The silver lining to this cloud was that it sparked off a massive reconstruction programme, at the very moment when Art Deco styles were taking root.

As a result, Miami has a splendid concentration of 1920s buildings, which are known collectively as the Deco District. This is a compact area of 80 blocks, centered on Flamingo Park, and it includes around 800 structures from the era of Art Deco contruction. The colorful nature of the architecture has made it a mecca for sightseers, and local authorities have organized guided tours of the district.

ART DECO DINER, MIAMI BEACH (C. 1935)

Courtesy of the Architectural Association / Sue Barr

Although at first glance it resembles a railway carriage that has somehow become stranded on a suburban street, this charming diner is one of the highlights of Miami's Deco District. It is situated on Collins Avenue, one block away from the celebrated Ocean Drive. The main structure itself is interesting enough, but the owners have also managed to preserve two ancillary features, which are absolutely typical of the Art Deco style. Above the entrance, the word "diner" is spelt out in *Broadway* lettering, the classic Art Deco typeface that was devstylized in 1929 by M. F. Benton. In addition, the wrought-iron railings at the top of the entry stairs feature a row of sunbursts. This is an archetypal Art Deco motif, which can be seen on the gateways of many 1930s houses in Britain.

Establishments of this kind, which one might normally expect to have only a limited life span, have been protected by Miami's diligent conservation authorities. Ironically, one of the principal tasks of these authorities has been to restrict modern architects from aping Art Deco styles too closely. It can be no coincidence, for example, that two leading fast-food chains have departed from their normal style and introduced Art Deco motifs into local outlets.

Hoover Factory, London (1932–35)
Wallis Gilbert and Partners
Courtesy of Edifice/Darley

This is Britain's most celebrated Art Deco building and, if it comes to that, probably its best-known factory. Few other styles of architecture could have transformed a humble place of work into the semblance of an exotic palace. The building was begun in 1932 by the firm of Wallis Gilbert and Partners. They already enjoyed a renowned reputation in this field, as they had previously designed a number of factories on the Great West Road leading out of London towards Bristol. This arterial route into the capital was sometimes known as the "Golden Mile", because it was lined with flourishing factories, most of which were constructed in the late 1920s and early 1930s. They were set back from the road, each with its own private lawn, and were specifically designed to appear imposing to the passing motorist. This was both an advantage and a drawback, since the very modernity of the designs raised the hackles of some influential figures. The architect Sir Nikolaus Bernhard Leon Pevsner (1902–83), for example, despised the Hoover Factory as "perhaps the most offensive of the modernistic atrocities along this road of typical bypass factories." Others shared this view and many of these palaces of industry were pulled down. Opinion began to shift only in 1980, after the demolition of the Firestone Building, Wallis Gilbert's other great masterpiece, which raised a public outcry.

HOOVER FACTORY, LONDON (1932–35)
Wallis Gilbert and Partners
Courtesy of Edifice/Darley

The reputation of the Hoover Factory is due largely to the careful balancing act it maintains between functionalism and rich decoration. On the one hand, it could be said to fulfil architect Le Corbusier's (Charles-Edouard Jeanneret, 1887–1965) dictum that all buildings "should be white by law." In addition, the simple geometric shapes of the main façade and the two staircase towers have a streamlined appearance, while the very large windows represented a genuine concession to the working conditions of Hoover's employees.

From the outside, it is the colorful details which catch the eye: such as bands of blue and red tiles, together with stylized sunbursts, and hints of neo-Egyptian pillars. Many sources of inspiration have been suggested—the corner windows on the towers are reminiscent of Erich Mendelsohn's (1887–1953) Einstein Tower in Potsdam (1921), while the tiling has some affinities with the Palais Stoclet (1905–11). The iron gates, meanwhile, have been compared to the Glasgow School of Art (1886–99), which was designed by Charles Rennie Mackintosh. Some of the Aztec and Egyptian motifs used were common currency in many branches of Art Deco design.

In spite of its unique qualities, the building was threatened with demolition when Hoover sold the property in the 1990s to a large supermarket chain. Luckily it was preserved by being named as a listed building; the exterior, and much of the interior, remains unspoilt.

BURGH ISLAND HOTEL, DEVON (1929)
Matthew Dawson (1875–1943)
Courtesy of Arcaid/Richard Bryant

There must have been something about the exuberant spirit of Art Deco which conjured up a holiday mood, for it is noticeable that, both in Britain and America, many of the finest examples of the style can be found in coastal resorts. The splendors of the exclusive Burgh Island Hotel, located just off the Devonshire coast, provide a case in point. As the illustration shows, the building was kitted out with the latest Art Deco accessories, right down to the ornaments on the reception desk. It was the interior, however, that won widest acclaim. The Palm Court, with its Peacock dome, wicker chairs and Modernist mirrors, was an uplifting sight. It remained accessible until 1984, when the building was converted into flats.

The architect, Matthew Dawson, had a varied career. After training at both the Ardrossan Academy and Sydney University, he joined the LCC (London County Council), where he was involved with the slum clearance programme. Through meetings at the Society for the Protection of Ancient Buildings, he also made the acquaintance of the architect Philip Speakman Webb (1831–1915). Dawson started up his own architectural practice in 1907 and, for a time, taught the subject at the Westminster Technical Institute.

INTERIOR, UNILEVER HOUSE, LONDON (1931–82)
Theo Crosby
Courtesy of Arcaid/Lucinda Lambton

Situated to the north of London's Blackfriars Bridge, Unilever House is a sparkling example of the way that Art Deco stylists could marry ancient and modern forms successfully. The building itself was built in 1930–31, to the designs provided by Sir John Burnet (1857–1938) working in conjunction with James Lomax-Simpson (1882–1977). It is notable, in particular, for its giant screen of columns and for the sculpted figures by William Read Dick.

Inside, the place comes alive. The lobby contains two very typical Art Deco features: the columns are inspired by the Egyptian Revival, which reached its peak in the late 1920s and early 1930s; these team up well with the chain of rectangular lightshades, adorned by jazzy Art Deco patterns. These geometric shapes are echoed by the lozenges in the flooring. In 1982, this interior was restored to its former glory by Theo Crosby, a key member of the Pentagram design team. Crosby retained the original features wherever possible, but added some new light fixtures, leaded glass, and ornamental metalwork. Pentagram, which was founded in 1972, has carried out similar projects elsewhere—the NMB Bank in Bijlmermeer, Amsterdam, Holland, is a typical example—but it remains best known for its work in the field of graphic design.

Michelin Building, London (1905–11)
François Espinasse
Courtesy of Edifice/Lewis

Situated just a few minutes away from the King's Road in London, this is one of the best-known architectural sights in fashionable Chelsea. It is a transitional building, blending some of the best features of the waning Art Nouveau style and the emerging trend for Art Deco. It was commissioned by Michelin, the tyre company, and designed by François Espinasse, a French architect from Clermont-Ferrand. The two-story structure has a recessed service bay at the front, surmounted by a large arched window. There are later extensions at the rear (1912 and 1922) and the building was sensitively restored by Conran Roche and YRM in 1985–86.

The chief focus of interest is the elaborate decoration, which covers much of the structure. It centers, in particular, on Bibendum, the tyre-man, who parades before us on his bicycle. This image may well be reminiscent of the cycling posters from the Art Nouveau era, but by the early 1900s, Michelin tyres were increasingly in use on motor cars, and these are also celebrated. No fewer than 34 brightly painted tiles can be found on the exterior, glorying in the victories achieved by racing-cars that had driven on Michelin tyres. The series of tiles was designed by Ernest Montaut, a leading poster artist, and was originally commissioned for Michelin's headquarters in Paris.

MICHELIN BUILDING (DETAIL), LONDON (1905–11)

François Espinasse

Courtesy of the Architectural Association / Paul Dawson

It is a measure of the air of confidence and stability in the pre-war society that so many companies commissioned tailor-made offices for themselves. In many cases, the ornamentation on their buildings reflected both the reputation and the products of their firm, blazoning them out to the world at large. It appears they believed that their company would occupy the site for perpetuity.

The Michelin Building typifies this trend: its walls are covered with references to the firm's products and past achievements. This particular detail shows a section of a frieze, featuring a row of wheels. It also includes a monogrammed plaque, containing the first few letters of the company's name. Similar motifs can be found on almost every part of the exterior. Bibendum, the tyre-clad company mascot, is depicted in several places, genially greeting the casual passer-by. Even the glass domes at the corner of the building are thought to represent piles of tires.

In spite of this catalogue of self-promotion, the Michelin company left the premises many years ago. The front part of the building housed a fashionable restaurant in the late 1990s, while the remainder was occupied by a design group, a publishing house, and an interior-design shop.

ROCKEFELLER CENTER, NEW YORK (1932–40)
Associated Architects
Courtesy of the Architectural Association/V. Bennett

The Rockefeller Center was a complex arts project that was eventually carried out by a consortium of architects. The original idea, conceived in 1927, was to provide a new home for the Metropolitan Opera Company. This notion came to the attention of John D. Rockefeller Junior, who volunteered to help. He negotiated the lease of the site with Columbia University and drew up a business plan, which would enable the opera house to be funded by the commercial development of the surrounding land. The Depression intervened, however, forcing the opera company to abandon the scheme. So, left with a sizable stretch of real estate in the middle of an economic crisis, Rockefeller had to come up with an alternative plan. In the end, he chose to develop America's first, large-scale urban renewal project.

The idea behind the original scheme dictated the piecemeal nature of the Rockefeller Center, which has often been described as "a city within a city." Amid the maze of shops and plazas, however, its focal point was the huge, 70-story RCA Building. This was principally the creation of Raymond Hood (1881–1934), the distinguished architect who had already created two of the finest Art Deco skyscrapers: the Chicago Tribune Tower (1923–25) and the American Radiator Company Building (1924).

ROOF GARDEN, ROCKEFELLER CENTER, NEW YORK (1932–40)
Associated Architects
Courtesy of the Architectural Association/Hazel Cook

From this viewpoint on Fifth Avenue, the Rockefeller Center really does appear to be a concrete jungle, with only a few square meters of token greenery to remind the inhabitants of the earth beneath their feet. The designers compensated for the rather austere appearance of the Center, however, by commissioning a plethora of Modernist *bas-reliefs* and panels. In addition to the carving of *Wisdom*, these included *The Joy of Life* (1937), a polychrome limestone panel by Attilio Piccrilli, a symbolic depiction of *Television* by Leo Friedlander, and three fine plaques by Hildreth Meiere, featuring spirited portrayals of *Song, Dance,* and *Drama*, all dating from 1932–40. The interior also contained lavish decorations, executed by a team of artists under the supervision of Donald Deskey (1894–1989).

The sheer scope of the Rockefeller project necessitated the involvement of a large group of architects. These included Corbett, Harrison & MacMurray; Hood, Godley & Fouilhoux; and Reinhard & Hofmeister. The overall development of the project was placed in the capable hands of Raymond Hood (1881–1934), who had already organized the construction of three other New York buildings: The American Radiator Company Building on West Street (1924), the *Daily News* Building (1929), and the McGraw-Hill Building (1930–32).

WISDOM (DETAIL), ROCKEFELLER CENTER, NEW YORK (1932–40)
Lee Lawrie
Courtesy of AKG Photo/Robert O'Dea

The buildings that make up the Rockefeller Center are certainly not the most attractive of New York's skyscrapers, but they can boast the finest decorations. Chief among them, perhaps, is this polychrome relief, which is featured above the entrance to the RCA Building. Executed by Lee Lawrie, it depicts the stern, patriarchal figure of Wisdom, gazing down at the customers who have come to enjoy a performance at the Center.

This illustration shows only a detail of the scene. In the full relief, Wisdom balances precariously on layers of stylized golden clouds (sections of three of these can be seen above the figure's right shoulder). With his right arm, he lowers a pair of compasses to point out the Center's motto: "Wisdom and Knowledge shall be the Stability of thy Times." Beneath this, there is a rectangular plaque with patterns of colored glass, created by the Steuben Glass Works, which was founded in 1903.

The image is loosely based on William Blake's (1757–1827) *The Ancient of Days*, which represented God the Father. The main difference lies in the heavy stylisations of Wisdom's beard, hair, and fingers. The beard, which flows up to the right as if caught in a powerful wind, is reminiscent of the car mascots produced by René Lalique (1860–1945) and others. These portrayed human heads, with their hair streaming out behind them, blown by the speed of the car.

MAYBURY DINER, EDINBURGH (1936)
Patterson and Broome
Courtesy of Arcaid/Nick Dawe

Although this building is classified as a diner, it is clearly a world away from the casual charm of the standard American eatery. Instead, it has the semblance of a luxurious hotel with a private ballroom. The diner's style is International Modernism at its most severe. Everything is strictly regulated, right down to the smallest lick of paint and the last pane of glass. Color is restricted. Black and white predominate, even with regard to the lighting in the car park. The only exception is the Maybury logo.

More importantly from an architectural point of view, there is a constant interplay between horizontals and verticals. The horizontal elements include the slats on the windows, the stripes above the ballroom entrance and the rings at the base of the forecourt lights, while the verticals consist of the windows above the main entrance, the flagpoles and the outside lamps.

Corner windows were extremely popular with Modernist architects, and the Maybury Diner is no exception. Very similar examples can be seen on Oliver Hill's housing complex at Frinton-on-Sea, and they are also in evidence at the Hoover Factory.

HOUSES, FRINTON-ON-SEA (1935)
Oliver Hill (1887–1968)
Courtesy of Edifice/Darley

The striking appearance of Oliver Hill's elegant row of houses in this coastal town forms a vivid contrast to the cosy, suburban look of their neighboring homes. The scheme is a prime example of the International Modern style, which followed the precept that all external decoration is superfluous. Buildings in this style tend to have plain surfaces, usually painted white; block-like silhouettes with flat roofs; and copious expanses of glass, held in place by horizontal, steel bands. Corner windows are also commonplace, and similar such features can be seen on the Maybury Diner and the Hoover Factory.

Oliver Hill was a prominent figure in the design world of the 1930s. In addition to his architectural work, he designed interior schemes, as well as individual pieces of furniture. He also appeared to be a permanent fixture at the scores of international exhibitions, which were staged at this period. He designed a stunning display for Pilkington Bros at the Dorland Hall Exhibition (1933), for example, and was also responsible for the British Pavilion at the 1937 Paris Exhibition. Of his own projects, the highlight was probably the refurbishment of the Morecombe Hotel (1932–33) on the west coast of England—a marvellous scheme, which included a mural by Eric Ravilious (1903–42).

De La Warr Pavilion, Bexhill (1933–35)
Mendelsohn & Chermayeff
Courtesy of the Architectural Association / Valerie Bennett

One of Britain's best Modernist buildings was designed by the two expatriate architects Serge Chermayeff (1900–96) and Erich Mendelsohn (1887–1953). Although Russian by birth, Chermayeff spent most of his life in England, becoming the director of the modern art department at Waring and Gillow. Mendelsohn was once a successful architect in his native Germany, but moved to England in 1933 to avoid the threat of Nazi persecution.

The two men went into partnership and, almost immediately, won a commission to design a new entertainment complex at the resort of Bexhill in East Sussex. The projected building was to have a prime site overlooking the sea. The finished design bore a strong resemblance to some of the schemes Mendelsohn had designed in the 1920s—most notably, the Universum Cinema (1925–28) in Berlin and the Schocken department store (1926) in Stuttgart. Its basic premise was simple. The left-hand section of the complex, which was to be the movie theater, required no natural daylight and could thus have an enclosed, box-like appearance; the right-hand section (the bar and cafeteria), on the other hand, would benefit from as many windows as possible. Linking these was the building's tour de force, a glazed semi-cylinder containing a massive spiral staircase.

BBC Broadcasting House, London (1931)
Val Myers & Watson-Hart
Courtesy of the Architectural Association/Paul Dawson

One of London's most familiar buildings, Broadcasting House owes its unusual shape not to the strictures of some Art Deco aesthetic, but rather to the very complicated nature of its site. It is on an awkward corner and the building had to follow the line of Nash's Regent Street scheme as well as blend in with the circular church of All Souls, which is beside the building. Despite this, the architects, Val Myers and Watson-Hart, made a virtue out of the problem and gave the building a unique prow-like frontage. Not everybody was pleased. Some critics dubbed the place "the new Tower of London," although it gained a place in the public's hearts during the Second World War, when it came to represent the spirit of national resistance.

The period interiors were designed by a number of well-known figures, such as Chermayeff, McGrath, and Wells Wintemute Coates (1895–1958), but most of these have since been removed. The feature that caused most controversy at the time was Eric Gill's (1882–1940) sculpture of *Prospero and Ariel*, situated prominently above the main entrance. The use of these Shakespearean characters to symbolize the medium of broadcasting was approved by the British Broadcasting Corporation, but the authorities were not pleased when they saw the results. The nude figure of Ariel—which was modelled on an actor named Leslie French, who had played the role on the stage—was deemed indecent, and modifications had to be made before the statues were unveiled.

GROSVENOR CINEMA, RAYNERS LANE, LONDON (1936)
F. E. Bromige
Courtesy of Edifice/Lewis

The movie theater was a comparatively new institution; the oldest surviving movie theater building in London, the Electric Cinema in Portobello Road, only dates back to 1910. Because of this, architects did not have to battle against public expectations of what a movie theater should look like. Instead, they followed the American practice of building sumptuous "movie palaces", where customers could escape for a few hours from the harsh realities of life. The choice of styles was remarkably varied, but the most memorable examples conjured up exotic cultures. The leading British architects in this field were George Coles, who created the Chinese-influenced Palace at Southall, west London (1929) and the streamlined elegance of the Gaumont in Kilburn, north London (1937), and Cecil Massey, who is best remembered for the Moorish fantasy of his movie theater in Northfields in the southwest of the city.

There are two surviving examples of Bromige's work in London: the former Grosvenor Cinema in Rayners Lane (now a wine bar) and the Dominion in Acton (1937). The Grosvenor demonstrates the architect's fondness for exuberant, neo-Baroque forms. The most striking feature is the huge volute, bisecting the frontage. This was meant to represent an elephant's trunk, and once supported a revolving triangular sign.

ARNOS GROVE STATION, LONDON (1932)
Adams, Holden & Pearson

Courtesy of the Architectural Association/Alan Chandler

In Britain, the scope for architectural innovation was always greatest when there was no clash of interest with other parties and when the public did not have a preconceived image of the building's appearance. In this respect, the new stations on the northern sections of the Tube network offered an ideal opportunity. The areas around Arnos Grove in north London were fairly sparsely populated and residents were only too pleased to see a new station in their area. Similarly, the piecemeal construction of the Tube system meant that it did not have a unified, corporate imagelike the Paris Metro. Accordingly, Charles Holden (1875–1960) was able to adopt a bold approach, when he designed the stations on the outer reaches of the Piccadilly Line. It was his belief that, as the trains themselves had a sleek Modernist look, it was only fitting that the stations themselves should have a simple, geometric appearance. Arnos Grove (1932) and Southgate (1935) are the best examples of this philosophy.

Holden had a very varied career. His early work included some designs for the Law Society Library and the British Medical Association, but he also became one of the chief architects of the Imperial War Graves Commission, designing no fewer than 67 cemeteries. In collaboration with Jacob Epstein (1880–1959), he also helped to design Oscar Wilde's extraordinary tomb in Paris (1909).

PENGUIN POOL, LONDON ZOO (1934)
Tecton

Courtesy of the Architectural Association / Valerie Bennett

The Penguin Pool at London Zoo is one of the most remarkable creations of the Russian architect, Berthold Lubetkin (1901–90). Born in Tiflis, Georgia, he studied with Auguste Perret (1874–1954) in Paris, where he absorbed the precepts of Le Corbusier. In 1930, he arrived in London and, with six young English architects, he founded the Tecton group. In the 1930s, this association became the leading exponent of the International Style in Britain.

One of Tecton's first major commissions was for a group of buildings at London Zoo. After completing the Gorilla House, they progressed to the most memorable part of the scheme. The interior of the pool combined genuine technical innovation with a stylish adaptation of Modernist elements. With the assistance of the engineer, Sir Ove Nyquist Arup (1895–1988), Lubetkin constructed two spiraling ramps, which intersected at the center of the pool. The intention was that the penguins could either use these as diving platforms or simply bask on them on sunny days. Structurally, the most interesting aspect of the design was the use of steel reinforcement—a genuine novelty in British architecture of this period. Visually, the meandering ramps gave the pool a chic, futuristic appearance, reminiscent of the Constructivist stage sets Lubetkin would have known from his native Russia.

GAS BOARD BUILDING, CROUCH END, LONDON (1937)

Courtesy of Edifice/Lewis

During the 1920s and 1930s, it was commonplace to decorate the rather plain walls of Modernist buildings with reliefs or sculptures. Obviously wherever possible, artists were encouraged to choose a theme that would be appropriate to the work carried out inside the structure.

In this instance, the sculpted plaque belongs to a complex of public buildings, centering on Hornsey Town Hall. The scheme was designed by R. H. Uren and the bulk of the construction work was completed in 1934–35. Set back from the Broadway in Crouch End, it consists of a tall brick tower together with a group of offices and shops surrounding a grass forecourt. The general layout of the scheme bears a passing resemblance to Willem Marinus Dudok's (1884–1974) Town Hall in Hilversum (1924–30). The results of the Hornsey project were highly regarded in official circles and Uren won a gold medal from the Royal Institution of British Architects.

One section of the ground-floor offices was occupied by the publicly owned Gas and Electricity Boards. Accordingly, this plaque was commissioned, in order to extol the benefits of gas. In her left hand, the woman holds a cornucopia, symbolizing abundance or plenty, while in her right hand she displays a jet of gas.

MI6 HEADQUARTERS, VAUXHALL CROSS, LONDON (1988–93)
Terry Farrell (b. 1938)
Courtesy of the Architectural Association/Paul Dawson

The taste for the drama and chic of Art Deco forms has resurfaced periodically since the 1930s. It has been particularly noticeable in recent years, perhaps because, as a style, Post-Modernism has proved to be every bit as eclectic as Art Deco. Hints of its influence can easily be discerned in the geometric simplifications and showy opulence of Terry Farrell's designs for the government offices at Vauxhall Cross.

The British architect Terry Farrell has enjoyed a growing reputation in recent years. He set up in partnership with Nicholas Grimshaw (b. 1939) in 1965, but branched out on his own in 1980. His earliest commissions were centered on London. In 1980–81, he was involved in the revamping of Covent Garden and he also won high praise for his imaginative redevelopment of the railway terminus at Charing Cross (1987–90). This stood him in good stead, when he won the commission to design Kowloon Railway Station in China (completed 1998), the largest undertaking of its kind in the world. Farrell's other work includes designs for the headquarters of Henley Regatta in Oxfordshire (1983–85) and for the television studios in Camden Town, London (1981–82).

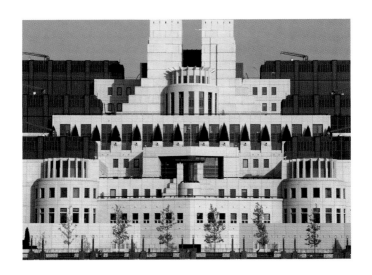

TOP HATS (POST-1930S)
Erté (1892–1990)

Christie's Images. Courtesy of The Bridgeman Art Library

Romain de Tirtoff was one of the leading designers of the Art Deco era. He was born in Russia, but moved to Paris in 1912 to study art at the Académie Julian. There, he adopted the name of Erté (the French pronunciation of his initials—R.T.). He remained in France and began working for Paul Poiret (1879–1944), where his skill as an illustrator soon attracted attention. He designed some covers for *Vogue*, but in 1915 he was poached by its fiercest rival, *Harper's Bazaar*. Over the next twenty years, he produced more than 240 cover designs and 2500 illustrations for the company. Erté was also a gifted costume and set designer. In this field, he produced work for both the George White Scandals and the Ziegfeld Follies in New York, while also enjoying a long association with the Folies Bergère. There, one of his greatest successes was with *Le Conte Hindou* (1921), for which he produced some of his most exotic and colorful costumes.

This particular image comes from a series entitled "The Twenties Remembered Again", in which Erté paid tribute to the glamor and the styles of the Art Deco era. Significantly, he used a backdrop of stylized skyscrapers—the most recognizable symbol of Art Deco architecture—just as Tamara de Lempicka did in so many of her paintings.

WOMAN DRESSED IN BLACK (1930s)
Erté (1892–1990)

Private Collection. Courtesy of The Bridgeman Art Library

No other Art Deco designer took stylisation to such extremes as Erté. This extraordinary concoction is pure fantasy. Viewed in isolation, the woman's face resembles that of an extra-terrestrial, with blue almonds for eyes and a cerise triangle for a mouth. Her stance is supremely elegant, even though it seems unlikely that she could hold it for any length of time. The combination of the dog, the unwieldy rolls of fur and the train of her dress would surely trip her up if she attempted to move.

Although the emphasis is clearly on the costume, it is worth stressing the importance of dogs in Art Deco designs. They feature as ornamental motifs in a wide range of artworks, though they are most closely associated with the small figurines made by such artists as Chiparus and Preiss. Dogs were regarded as genuine fashion accessories at the time: actresses would arrive at Hollywood premiers with two or three of them, and they figured prominently in fashion illustrations. Only a few select types of dog, however, were suitable for this purpose. These were the breeds with sleek, elegant lines—borzois, salukis, Afghans, and, above all, grayhounds. It was emphatically not the done thing to be seen in public with a mere terrier or hound.

COSTUME DESIGN FOR GABY DESLYS
(C. 1918)
Erté (1892–1990)

Private Collection. Courtesy of The Bridgeman Art Library

Gaby Deslys (1883–1920) was one of the most famous music-hall stars of her day. Born in Marseilles, she made her reputation in the US, performing in a number of Broadway shows. These included *Vera Violetta* (1911), in which she invented a dance called "the Gaby Glide"; *Honeymoon Express* (1913), where she co-starred with Al Jolson; and *The Belle of Bond Street* (1914).

In 1917, Deslys made a triumphant return to Paris, opening at the Casino de Paris in *Laissez-le Tomber!* ("Drop him!") She was now performing the American jazz numbers that she had learnt in New York—a style of music that was entirely unknown in Paris and that would make even more of an impact after Josephine Baker's arrival, a few years later. French audiences were dazzled by Deslys's show, partly on account of the music—which Cocteau described as "a hurricane of rhythm and drumbeats", mixed in with saxophones, car horns, and gunshots—and partly on account of Gaby's appearance. She came on stage with her hair dyed blonde, in a dress decked out with ostrich feathers and plumes, and wearing jewels that had been given to her by the King of Portugal. For all her success Deslys died young, leaving most of her money to the poor of Marseilles.

LA PARESSE (1924–25)
George Barbier (1882–1932)

Collection Archiv F. Kunst & Geschichte Berlin. Courtesy of AKG Photo

This scene of cultured decadence is by the French graphic artist, George Barbier. It is a *pochoir* print, based on a watercolor of 1924; it appeared in a fashion annual *Falbalas et Fanfreluches* the following year. This magazine made a practice of instructing its artists to produce themed series of illustrations. Here, Barbier offers us his version of *Sloth*, one of the vices depicted in a series illustrating the seven deadly sins.

The scene is set in a type of harem, where two very modern odalisques lounge on a rich array of carpets and cushions. The birds in the background appear to be based on the traditional image of the phoenix, but they are more likely to have been inspired by the currently fashionable image of the firebird—the magical bird of Russian folklore and the subject of Stravinsky's controversial ballet, which had taken Paris by storm in 1910. Other elements are typical of the Art Deco period: the huge table-lamp; the women's short, bobbed hairstyles; and, most of all, the slender cigarette-holder, which had become the latest word in fashionable self-indulgence. The discarded book harks back to older representations of *Sloth*, in which artists were more likely to focus on mental inactivity than physical laziness.

LE SOIR (1925–26)
George Barbier (1882–1932)

Collection Archiv F. Kunst & Geschichte Berlin. Courtesy of AKG Photo

This extraordinary scene was published in the 1926 edition of the fashion almanac, *Falbalas et Fanfreluches*. It is based on a George Barbier watercolor, executed in the previous year. In the most exotic of interiors, a young man goes down on one knee to declare his love for a modish beauty. In typical Barbier fashion, the man's features are effeminate, and he appears to be wearing eye-shadow and rouge, while the woman displays an air of sublime hauteur, as if the least show of affection will somehow ruffle her costume.

Hard though it is to look away from this central image, the other accessories in the room underline the eclectic roots of Art Deco. The statue on the left confirms the popularity of African tribal art in the early years of the century. This had exerted a huge influence on Picasso's early style, most notably in his celebrated *Les Demoiselles d'Avignon* (1906–07), and it was one of the basic components of Cubism. The impact of these artworks was particularly strong in France, which still ruled over a number of African colonies. In the background, Barbier has included a sumptuous lacquer screen, a typical example of the oriental influence apparent in Art Deco works. Jean Dunand (1877–1942) produced many screens of this kind in the 1920s, created by using traditional techniques.

INCANTATION (1922–23)
George Barbier (1882–1932)
Collection Archiv F. Kunst & Geschichte Berlin. Courtesy of AKG Photo

This is one of Barbier's many designs for the fashion almanac *Falbalas et Fanfreluches*. His original watercolor of this design was executed in 1922 and the illustration appeared in print in the following year. Barbier was a regular contributor to the publication, particularly during the years between 1922 and 1926. As usual, his illustration takes the form of a vignette of social life, showing two women performing a song, while a dapper but effeminate man looks on. The ladies have fashionably short haircuts. Women's hairstyles became increasingly severe as the decade drew on, progressing from the bob to the shingle, and, finally, the Eton crop. In *Incantation*, their evening gowns are low-waisted and display the tubular, "barrel line", the long, lean, flat style which was popular at that time.

Like so many of his fellow Art Deco designers, Barbier was extremely versatile, producing work in a number of different fields. Among other things, he designed wallpaper, book illustrations, and costumes for the stage as well as the movie theater. He was particularly fond of ballet, designing some of his finest illustrations for the *Danses de Nijinsky* (1913), and there is no doubt that his fashion scenes were influenced by the costumes of the Ballets Russes.

L'ORGUEIL (1924–25)
George Barbier (1882–1932)
Collection Archiv F. Kunst & Geschichte Berlin. Courtesy of AKG Photo

This beguiling picture appeared in the almanac *Falbalas et Fanfreluches, Almanach des modes...pour 1925*, a French fashion album that was published annually. *L'Orgueil* is based on a watercolor by George Barbier, executed in 1924, and it forms part of a series of illustrations on the seven deadly sins. The scene represents *Pride*, and it is a companion piece to *Sloth*.

As in the case of *Sloth*, Barbier has chosen to endow the vice with a decidedly oriental flavor. The exotic headdress may have been inspired by Leon Bakst's (1866–1924) extraordinary designs for the Ballets Russes—whose performances of *Cléopatra* (1909) and *Schéhérazade* (1910) exerted a lasting influence on Parisian fashion and design. Both Barbier and Erté produced illustrations of dresses entitled *Schéhérazade* and the Casino de Paris staged a glittering revue entitled *The Persian Carpet* (1920). Other possible sources of inspiration may have been provided by *Salomé*, Strauss's operatic setting of the Oscar Wilde play, or even the Folies Bergère. The background detail in this print is slightly ambiguous, but it might be interpreted as a battery of spotlights, about to focus on the exotic dancer. This would accord well with the striptease element and would also be appropriate for the theme of vanity.

L'Eau (1925–6)
George Barbier (1882–1932)

Collection Archiv F. Kunst & Geschichte Berlin. Courtesy of AKG Photo

This is another of Barbier's designs for a fashion annual. His original watercolor version was executed in 1925 and, in the following year, this version was published in *Falbalas et Fanfreluches, Almanach des modes...pour 1926*. As with so many fashion plates, both publisher and artist tried to vary the formula by looking for a theme to link the pictures. This particular image is one of a series illustrating the Four Elements.

Bathing costumes evolved dramatically in the 1920s and 1930s, becoming considerably more skimpy. In part, this was due to increasingly liberal attitudes and the new role of women, but it also had something to do with the practice of sunbathing. It was this, rather than bathing itself, which gained new levels of popularity during the Art Deco era. There was a widespread belief that exposure to sunshine was beneficial for the health. It followed, therefore, that sunbathers should expose as much flesh as possible.

Stylistically, George Barbier's print draws on a number of sources. In particular, there are echoes of the Japanese woodcut prints that had introduced decorative, curvilinear effects into Western art in the second half of the 19th century. This influence is most evident in the stylized foliage in the background.

My Wife with a Gramophone (1927)
Kurt Weinhold
Rolf Deyhle Collection, Stuttgart. Courtesy of AKG Photo

One of the most shocking fashion statements of the 1920s was the short skirt. By the mid-1920s, this had reached levels that were unprecedented in the West, and which would not be seen again until the advent of the mini skirt in the 1960s. Predictably, the media had a field day, as cartoonists fantasized mischievously about the possible effect that these outrageous garments would have on more conventional members of the public. In deeply conservative areas, the reaction was one of disgust rather than amusement. The Archbishop of Naples blamed an earthquake on the justifiable wrath of God directed against the immorality of a society that permitted the wearing of skirts that rose more than three inches above the ankle.

The development of the short skirt can be linked to the ever-increasing emancipation of women, which resulted in skimpier and less restrictive clothing. There was also, however, a more practical reason for the change. Dancing had become one of the most popular pastimes of the era, and short dresses made it easier to carry out some of the more energetic moves required by modern dances such as the charleston.

COCO CHANEL IN A PURPLE OUTFIT (C. 1930)
Sir Cecil Beaton (1904–80)
Courtesy of The Bridgeman Art Library

Gabrielle Bonheur Chanel (1883–1971), better known as Coco, was one of the leading couturiers of the Art Deco period. Born in Saumur, France, her first sally into the fashion business was as a millinery specialist, operating from a tiny shop in Paris. Before the outbreak of the First World War, she had progressed to making dresses, which she sold in her new outlets: in the fashionable resorts of Biarritz and Deauville. The key to her success lay in her use of simple, lightweight fabrics, which offered her clients an unprecedented freedom of movement. This appealed greatly to the new generation of women: one that had won the vote and was breaking into many areas of the previously male-dominated world. For them, the heavy corsetry and bustles of the preceding era symbolized the mental as well as physical restrictions that had been placed on them, and they were delighted to cast them aside. Chanel was also instrumental in introducing the trend for costume jewelry, which became enormously popular during the 1920s.

With his characteristic wit, Beaton's portrayal of Chanel depicts her outfit in some detail and includes her scissors—the tools of her trade—but surprisingly for a portrait photographer neglects to show her face. This emphasizes the fact that the name "Chanel" has become wholly associated with the world of fashion, not with Coco Chanel as a person. Beaton himself was a theater and fashion designer, although he is best remembered for his photographic work. He eventually became the official photographer for the British royal family.

THE WEDDING MARCH (1929)
Georges Lepape (1887–1971)

Private Collection. Courtesy of The Bridgeman Art Library

As a magazine of international standing, *Vogue* helped to transmit the styles and ideas of Art Deco designers around the Western world. American *Vogue* had been established in the early 1890s, at the height of the Art Nouveau boom. In the early years of the 20th century, it began to lose some of its cutting edge, until it was acquired by Condé Nast in 1909. Through Nast's entrepreneurial skills, the magazine began to flourish once again and European offshoots were founded. British *Vogue* began publication in 1916—after German submarines disrupted the supply of magazines from the US— and a French version followed in 1920. From then until the late 1920s, American *Vogue* imported many of its graphics from Europe, and this helped to popularize the Modernist influences of Art Deco in the United States. The US did not participate at the 1925 Paris Exhibition and remained lukewarm about some aspects of Art Deco until comparatively late.

Over the years, Georges Lepape designed an impressive array of covers for *Vogue*. Even so, he will always be best known for his work with the Ballets Russes and his collaboration with Paul Poiret. In particular, it was his illustrations for *Les Choses de Paul Poiret* that secured his reputation.

ADVERTISEMENT FOR WEIL FURS (C. 1920)
Georges Lepape (1887–1971)

Private Collection. Courtesy of The Bridgeman Art Library

In addition to their work for couturiers, fashion illustrators also produced straightforward publicity material for retailers. This advertisement was produced for a well-known furrier, Weils of Paris. Rather surprisingly, the clients have decided to promote the functional aspect of their garments rather than market them as a mere fashion statement. It is a chill winter's day and snow is falling. As the lady enters her home, two winged cherubs, representing winds, assail her with their frozen breath. As the company promises, however, she feels nothing. The caption reads: "Tout vous est aquillon. Tout me semble zéphyr..." which, loosely translated, means: "What feels to you like a cold north wind, appears to me like a gentle, summer breeze." Despite this emphasis on the warmth of the fur, however, the inclusion of the stylish car and the carpeted steps (implying that the wearer lives in an expensive apartment) reinforce the impression that Weil's customers are wealthy and have impeccable taste.

Georges Lepape was one of the leading figures in fashion illustration at this time. He studied under both Humbert and Cormon—the latter also taught both Henri de Toulouse-Lautrec (1864–1901) and Henri Matisse (1869–1954)—and his varied training enabled him to apply his talent in many fields. In addition to fashion material, Lepape designed posters, book illustrations, and stage sets.

Tout vous est aquilon. Tout me semble zéphyr...

...grâce aux
Fourrures de

WEIL

PARIS :: 4, Rue Sainte-Anne, 4 :: PARIS

UNE MINUTE, ET JE SUIS PRÊTE (1924–25)
Georges Lepape (1887–1971)

Victoria and Albert Museum. Courtesy of E.T. Archive

In comparison with the fantasies of George Barbier, this is a fairly conventional fashion plate. It was designed by Georges Lepape and published in the 1924–25 edition of *La Gazette du Bon Ton*. This was one of the most sumptuous fashion magazines of the period. In its comparatively brief life (1912–25), it set new standards in illustration and assembled a formidable array of contributors—among them Robert Bonfils, Umberto Brunelleschi, and Erté.

Lepape's only concession to the *Gazette's* trendier rivals was the picture's humorous caption. The comment, "Une minute et je suis prête" ("I'll be ready in a minute") scarcely seems to accord with the unhurried manner of these two ladies. The clothes illustrated here were actual designs by Jeanne Lanvin (1867–1946), one of the top couturiers of the period. She was born in Brittany, but moved to Paris in the mid-1890s, where she began her career as a milliner. She then specialized in designing children's clothes, before turning her attention to high fashion. Lanvin became renowned for her soft, feminine style, although she adapted well to the more boyish *gamin* look of the 1920s. The House of Lanvin remained in business after her death, providing a showcase for the talents of Antonio del Castillo and Jules-François Crahay.

"UNE MINUTE, ET JE SUIS PRÊTE..."

ROBE ET MANTEAU DU SOIR, DE JEANNE LANVIN

N° 5 de la Gazette.

Année 1924-1925. — Planch

Modèles déposés. Reproduction interdite.

SUMMERTIME (1920s)
Paul Poiret (1879–1944)
John Jesse, London. Courtesy of The Bridgeman Art Library

This illustration of designs by Molyneux and Poiret was published in *Art-Goût-Beauté*, one of the leading fashion magazines of the day. Captain Edward Molyneux (1891–1974) was a British designer, who began his career as a freelance illustrator for magazines and newspapers. After serving as a captain in the First World War, he moved to Paris and turned his hand to fashion design. By 1929, he had outlets in a number of major fashion centers, including Cannes, Biarritz, and Monte Carlo.

Paul Poiret was a more celebrated figure, who also did much to shape the course of fashion in the 1920s. He worked for both Jacques Doucet (1853–1929) and The House of Worth, before opening his own fashion house in 1904. He met Josef Hoffmann and, inspired by his example, founded the Atelier Martine (1911), which designed a wide range of goods, including wallpapers, rugs, and textiles. More than anyone else, Poiret is thought to be responsible for the loose-fitting, highly colorful fashions of the Art Deco period. He also created a new benchmark for fashion illustration, after promoting his work through a series of lavish brochures: the most influential of these were *Les Robes de Paul Poiret* (1908) and *Les Choses de Paul Poiret*. Much of his inspiration apparently may have come from Bakst's costumes for the Ballets Russes, although Poiret was swift to deny this.

Art - Goût - Beau

WRISTWATCH, PENDANT, AND BROOCH (C. 1925)
Linzeler and Marchak
Courtesy of Christie's Images

Art Deco jewelry comes in a bewildering variety of forms: from the severe and geometric through to Egyptian and Oriental themes. The most prestigious jewelers—Cartier, Van Cleef & Arpels, Fouquet, Boucheron—made extensive use of precious stones, but it was acceptable to wear items adorned with brightly-colored enamels, even though these were cheap and mass-produced.

Ladies' wristwatches tended to be very narrow and slender, often with a rectangular dial. This example, by the firm of Linzeler and Marchak, is composed of diamonds, emeralds, and enamel. Necklaces with pendants or tassels were worn very long, sometimes reaching the stomach. This, combined with a short skirt, was the essential costume for dancing. The geometric brooch is by Jean Fouquet. His father, Georges, was also a jeweler and Jean joined the family firm in 1919. At the height of the Art Deco period, he made a speciality of understated circular pieces, in which he combined coral or onyx with tiny diamonds. Fouquet exhibited at the Salon d'Automne and, in 1930, became one of the founder members of the Union des Artistes Modernes. He continued to design jewelry until the 1960s.

A Selection of Art Deco Jewelry (1920s)
Louis Cartier (1819–1904)

Courtesy of Christie's Images

The name of Cartier had long enjoyed an unparalleled reputation in the field of jewelry, and it adapted well to the new styles which emerged during the Art Deco years. The firm had been founded in 1847 by Louis-François Cartier, who collaborated closely with the great couturier Charles Worth. Alfred Cartier (1841–1925) took over the business in 1874, and he in turn was joined by his son, Louis-Joseph (1875–1942), who masterminded the company's subsequent rise. He had a passion for diamonds and believed that their impact would be greatest if the settings were simple and understated.

Louis's determination to set his firm apart from the competition became very evident at the Paris Exhibition of 1925. He declined to display his creations alongside other jewelry designers. Instead, Cartier exhibited in the Pavillon d'Elégance, together with the fashion designs of couturier Jeanne Lanvin (1867–1946). With mannequins based on drawings by Constantin Brancusi (1876–1957) and Amedeo Modigliani (1884–1920), the combination of haute couture and jeweled accessories proved one of the great talking points of the show, enhancing Cartier's reputation still further. This illustration shows a selection of the firm's designs from the 1920s. They include a lavish bracelet; a pair of clips, studded with diamonds and sapphires; a diamond brooch; and an Art Deco ring.

VANITY CASE (1920s)
Cartier
Courtesy of Christie's Images

In November 1922, archaeologist Howard Carter reached the summit of his career, when he finally located Egypt's tomb of King Tutankhamen in the Valley of the Kings. The initial discoveries in the antechamber, which included golden amulets, cult figures, and ceremonial weapons, caught the attention of the world's media. Excitement then mounted as, over the next few months, the excavations extended to the royal chamber, where the boy king lay buried in a coffin made of solid gold. This, coupled with growing rumors about a mystical curse, which was said to be claiming the lives of those involved in the expedition, held the public spellbound. Not surprisingly, it triggered off a craze for all things Egyptian, which affected every branch of the arts.

Egyptian motifs were featured in Art Deco furniture, in contemporary fashions, in architectural details, and in the graphic arts. With this particular item, Cartier borrowed a familiar image from ancient hieroglyphics and placed it in a modern setting. In creating the box, he used a variety of precious materials, such as lapis lazuli, coral, emeralds, diamonds, and enamel. These were intended to complement the exotic flavor of the inset tablet.

SCARAB BROOCHES (1920s)

Courtesy of Christie's Images

The Egyptian revival of the 1920s left its mark on all walks of life. It transformed offices, factories, and movie theaters into imitation temples from the Luxor Valley, and it encouraged fashion-conscious women to go about in public wearing copies of grave-goods from a pharaoh's tomb. In almost every case, designers followed two cardinal rules: first, they made no attempt to translate any of the religious or symbolic meanings of the original artefact into the new creation; in addition, they did not hesitate to modify the design, by adding motifs or materials from entirely different cultures.

The scarab or dung-beetle was sacred to the ancient Egyptians. They regarded it as a symbol of Khepri, the sun-god of Heliopolis. This stemmed from a belief that the beetle was generated spontaneously from a circular ball of dung, resembling the sun. As a result, *faïence* depictions of scarabs were widely used as amulets. The living wore them for protection, but they were more commonly associated with funeral rites. During the rituals performed after death, a scarab amulet would be placed over the heart of the deceased, in the hope that Khepri would intercede on the soul's behalf when the moment to face judgment came.

A SELECTION OF FASHION ACCESSORIES (1920s)

Courtesy of Christie's Images

At the height of the Art Deco boom, cosmetics and other accessories became as bright and gaudy as the fashions themselves. The most sumptuous of the pictured items is a nephrite and enamel bangle, which is encrusted with diamonds (top left). Below it and to the right, there are jabot pins, featuring stylized representations of a rose and a dragon; these are decorated with tiny diamonds. The remaining items are a lipstick holder and a vanity case.

The most salient feature of these accessories is their sheer eclecticism. The bangle, for example, is recognizably based on Celtic models. The ancient Gauls and other Celtic peoples wore torcs (neck-bands) and armlets with similar animal-head terminals as seen here. These had been re-popularized at the turn of the century, when shops such as Liberty's marketed a range of Celtic jewelry. One difference was that the original bangles were usually made out of bronze or gold, while the Art Deco examples were highly colored and adorned with jewels.

The stepped pattern, which figures on the edges of the vanity case, carries similar overtones of ancient history. The motif probably derived from Babylonian ziggurats or Mayan pyramids; the geometric simplicity of the design appealed greatly to Art Deco designers and this style of decoration was featured on a wide variety of contemporary jewelry.

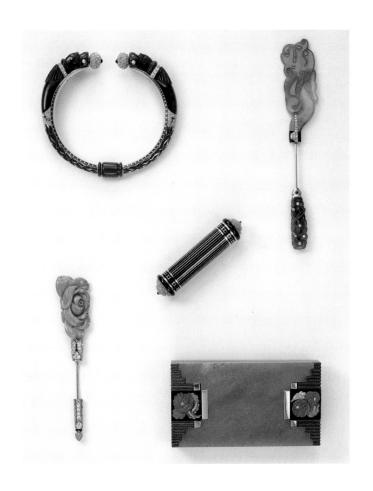

A SELECTION OF BROOCHES, WATCHES, RINGS AND EARRINGS

Courtesy of Christie's Images

The changing face of fashion had major repercussions for jewelry design. The taste for severe geometric shapes, for instance, caused practical difficulties for watchmakers. Often, the dials were so narrow that it was impossible to space out the numerals evenly. In one of the pictured examples, ten of the digits have had to be squeezed in vertically. Some designers chose to make a feature of this, as Preiss did in his *Thoughts*, when he enlarged the "six" and the "12", but there was generally insufficient room for this on a watch.

To compensate for the shorter haircuts, there was a vogue for long, dangling earrings. Many of the fashion plates illustrated in this book confirm the trend, the most extreme example being an advertisement for Weil Furs. Tassel earrings became equally popular, as their shimmering movement became an eye-catching feature, when the wearer was walking or dancing. Changes in the materials worn by women also had an impact on design. After the First World War, there was a growing taste for light fabrics, such as muslin or rayon, and these could not readily support the heavy jewelry that had been popular in the Art Nouveau era. Brooches, in particular, were often quite tiny, and they were as likely to be pinned to a hat or belt as to a dress.

SLEEPING WOMAN (1935)
Tamara de Lempicka (1898–1980)
Private Collection. Courtesy of AKG Photo

Tamara de Lempicka was one of the most gifted painters of the Art Deco period. After settling in Paris, she established a reputation as the most fashionable portraitist of the day, drawing her clientele from the cream of society. Writers, film stars, and foreign nobility all clamored for her services. *Sleeping Woman* was painted at one of the happiest junctures of her life, not long after her second marriage and when her popularity was at its peak.

In common with Jean Dupas (1882–1964), Lempicka evolved a very distinctive female type in her paintings. Inspired by the so-called "tubism" of Fernand Léger, her women have rounded, tubular limbs and skin that is so smooth that it almost appears metallic. In many of her paintings, these curvaceous qualities were offset by a geometric background, composed of tilting skyscrapers, but in this picture there is no such contrast. The girl's hair and the rumpled sheets have the same metallic sheen as her complexion. Despite some superficial similarities, there is a pronounced difference between the nudes of Dupas and Lempicka. His women have a neutral, asexual air, which accords well with their role as elements of decoration. On the other hand, Lempicka—who was bisexual—endowed her female models with a pronounced erotic charge.

SELF-PORTRAIT (TAMARA IN THE GREEN BUGATTI) (1925)
Tamara de Lempicka (1898–1980)

Private Collection, Paris. Courtesy of AKG Photo

This is one of the defining images of the Art Deco period. It has all the ingredients which gave the age its distinctive spirit of exuberance: a beautiful woman, free and in control of her own destiny; and a love of machinery and, in particular, of stylish cars; a devotion to all that was chic, glamorous, and expensive. That this is a carefully constructed fantasy world is borne out by the fact that the artist never actually owned a green Bugatti. Instead, she drove a modest yellow Renault. However, Lempicka voiced her reasons for this self-portrait in the following words: "The important thing was that I always dressed like the car, and the car like me."

The picture was commissioned for the cover of *Die Dame*, a German fashion magazine. It proved a great success and was hailed as the perfect embodiment of the modern, emancipated woman. Fifty years later, it fulfilled a similar role for the feminist movement, described in 1974 by a journalist writing about the picture in *Auto-Journal*: "She is wearing gloves and a helmet. She is inaccessible, a cool disconcerting beauty, behind which a formidable being can be glimpsed—this woman is free!"

ANDROMEDA (1929)
Tamara de Lempicka (1898–1980)
Private Collection. Courtesy of AKG London

The plight of Andromeda is a familiar story taken from the Roman poet Ovid's *Metamorphoses*. Andromeda was an Ethiopian princess, the daughter of King Cepheus. Because of Andromeda's mother's overly proud boasts about her daughter's beauty, the god Jupiter ordered the princess to be chained to a rock and sacrificed to a sea monster. At this very moment, Perseus flew by, fresh from his mission to kill the Gorgon Medusa, borne aloft by his winged sandals. Spying the maiden from afar, he swooped down and was instantly struck by Andromeda's beauty. "You should not be wearing such chains as these," he called out to her. "The only fit bonds for you are those which bind the hearts of true lovers." He proceeded to slay the beast and carry the princess off as his bride.

The legend had been a popular subject for artists ever since the Renaissance. Initially, the main focus was on the airborne warrior, but gradually it shifted towards the woman. Lempicka's immediate source was probably Ingres' painting of *Roger and Angelica* (an almost identical story), dating from 1819. As in Ingres' version, the main spotlight in *Andromeda* is on the nude female victim; this is emphasized by the artist choosing to leave Perseus's name out of the picture's title.

In Lempicka's canvas, the figure of Andromeda is placed in a definitively modern setting and against a Cubist cityscape. Another innovation is the prominence of the heavy manacles, which conjure up an air of decadence and sexual role-playing. These in turn raise the question as to whether this Andromeda is a victim or a temptress.

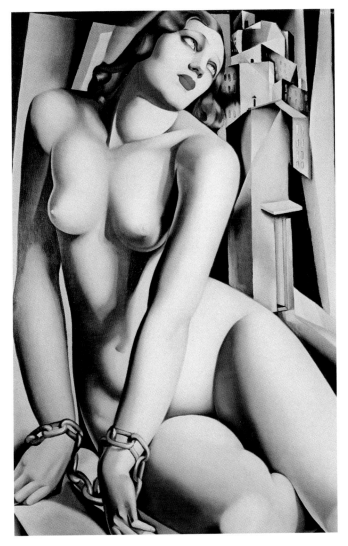

New York (c. 1930–35)
Tamara de Lempicka (1898–1980)
Private Collection. Courtesy of The Bridgeman Art Library

Tamara de Lempicka (*née* Gorska) was born in Warsaw, the Polish capital, but left the country when she married a Russian lawyer. In 1918, following the Russian Revolution, they fled to the West and settled in Paris. There, Lempicka studied painting under Maurice Denis (1870–1943) and André Lhote (1885–1962). From the former, she derived the decorative, curvilinear aspect that became a defining aspect of her style, while the latter, as a pioneer of Cubism, taught her more about the latest Modernist developments. Lempicka did not travel to New York until the Depression but, even in those straitened times, she was struck by the vigor of the place. That energy and the conflicting influences of her early life and artistic training can be discerned in this painting. She eventually settled in America, living mainly in Houston (1963–78), before moving to Mexico (1978–80), where she died.

This cityscape of New York is not typical of Lempicka's work. Normally she painted portraits, figure subjects, and, occasionally, still lifes. She did, however, frequently use skyscrapers and other rectangular shapes as backdrops for her portraits, and it may be that this was a practice piece for one of those. In true Cubist fashion, the picture does not represent a realistic scene—the contours of the buildings overlap and different viewpoints are employed. The skyscrapers—defining symbols of New York—are components in a fragmented, geometric pattern.

STREET, NEW YORK NO. 1 (1926)
Georgia O'Keeffe (1887–1986)
Private Collection. Courtesy of AKG Photo

After their marriage in December 1924, O'Keeffe and the art dealer Alfred Stieglitz settled in New York. For the first few months they lived in their studio on 58th Street, but in November 1925 they moved to an apartment in the newly-built Shelton Hotel on Lexington Avenue. Their home was on the 28th floor, which proved a remarkable experience for O'Keeffe. "I had never lived up so high before, and was so excited that I began talking about trying to paint New York. Of course, I was told that it was an impossible idea—even the men had not done too well with it."

Ultimately, however, O'Keeffe's pictures of the city are among her finest work, and they come closer than any of her other paintings to capturing the spirit of the Art Deco style. Although she painted a number of sweeping panoramas, reproducing the spectacular view from her apartment, the most successful pictures were painted at street level. These convey the sheer scale of the skyscrapers by adopting a snail's-eye view of the scene. This technique exaggerates both the length and the height of the buildings, giving the viewer the impression of passing through a steep gorge. O'Keeffe adds to this effect by squeezing the sky—the very epitome of boundless space—into a narrow, confined strip of canvas.

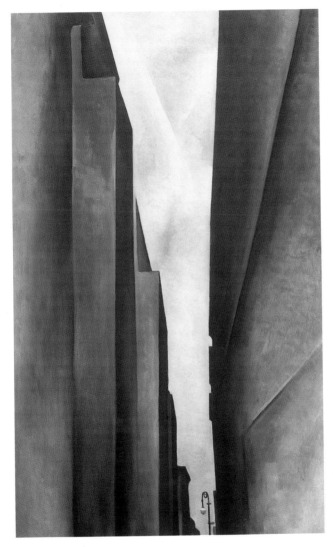

MOON IN NEW YORK (1925)
Georgia O'Keeffe (1887–1986)
Thyssen-Bornemisza Collection, Madrid. Courtesy of AKG Photo

Georgia O'Keeffe's paintings of New York are paeans to the beauty of the modern city, to the glories of the man-made landscape. Nature may have its wonders, but the tiny moon in this evening sky appears quite unimpressive, bedded on its ripple of feathery clouds. It pales into insignificance beside the city's "moons"—the haloed light of the street-lamp and the red glow of the traffic signs.

This was one of O'Keeffe's earliest city scenes, and she was extremely pleased with it. She wanted her art-dealer husband, Alfred Stieglitz, to feature it in his new show, "Seven Americans", which was due to open in March 1925. In the end, however, the picture was not displayed. O'Keeffe was furious, believing that the male artists in the exhibition were jealous and had persuaded him to exclude it. Another possible reason was that Stieglitz was introducing her large flower-pieces in "Seven Americans" and did not want anything to divert the critics' attention away from them. Whatever the truth of the matter, O'Keeffe was insistent that the picture should be included in his next exhibition, in February 1926. There, her confidence in the painting was fully vindicated: "It sold on the very first day of the show; the very first picture sold. From then on, they let me paint New York."

LAKE GEORGE (1923)
Georgia O'Keeffe (1887–1986)
Private Collection. Courtesy of The Bridgeman Art Library

Georgia's visits to Lake George began after she met her future husband, Alfred Stieglitz (1864–1946), the celebrated photographer and art dealer. Stieglitz's family had been renting a succession of summer cottages there since the 1870s, eventually purchasing a permanent home, Oaklawn, in 1886. Stieglitz gave O'Keeffe her first one-woman show in 1917 and, in the following year, his mother invited Georgia down to Oaklawn for the summer. This became a regular occurrence, as the couple continued their lengthy courtship. They eventually married in 1924.

Lake George had many positive and romantic associations for O'Keeffe. Nevertheless, she was a very private person, used to living a spartan and solitary existence, and the sheer size and intrusiveness of Stieglitz's family was sometimes overwhelming. As a result she took every opportunity to work by herself. She became an enthusiastic gardener, and enjoyed painting landscapes and even vegetables at quiet corners of the lake.

This tranquil scene is typical of many artists' approaches to nature in the 1920s. The radical surgery of the Cubists has left its mark, most notably in the stylized forms and simplified colors. This is most evident in the pleated lines of the sky, which might indicate menacing clouds or gusting winds. Either way, they inject a note of dynamism into the composition.

EGGPLANT (1924)
Georgia O'Keeffe (1887–1986)

Art Gallery of Ontario, Toronto. Courtesy of The Bridgeman Art Library

Art Deco designers drew inspiration from the host of avant-garde art movements which sprang up in the first two decades of the century. In the case of Georgia O'Keeffe, the main source of interest was her Precisionism, a style that she pioneered along with Charles Demuth (1883–1935) and also Charles Sheeler (1883–1965). In essence, this entailed the depiction of objects or townscapes in a sharply focused, highly realistic manner. Human figures were absent, colors were extremely vivid, and both social comment and narrative detail were excluded.

In general, the Precisionists preferred to apply their style to urban or industrial subjects. O'Keeffe was no exception, and her views of New York are probably her finest achievements in this field. However, she also painted a series of fruit and flowers in a similar manner. These were usually viewed from very close up, so that the objects assumed monumental proportions. In some instances—particularly in the flower-pieces—only part of the item was portrayed, lending the image a certain ambiguity. When suitably magnified, the folds and frills of individual petals seemed to suggest parts of the human anatomy. This portrayal of an aubergine is one of O'Keeffe's more conservative efforts, but the close viewpoint is still unsettling (it is not immediately obvious, for example, in which direction the floor is located) and the extreme clarity of the handling gives the object a strange, almost hallucinogenic quality.

FLAMENCO DANCERS (C. 1935)
Edward Burra (1905–76)
Whitford & Hughes, London. Courtesy of The Bridgeman Art Library

One of the most pervasive features of Art Deco design was a taste for the exotic. Time and again, artists would incorporate motifs from distant times or faraway places—places they had never visited and times they could not have seen—to give their work a romantic flavor. Conversely, Edward Burra was not content with historical or fantastical influences, he was determined to seek out the exotic locations for himself and to record them in his own inimitable fashion. In part, this was an act of rebellion against his upbringing. For Burra came from a well-to-do household, based in the sleepy coastal town of Rye in East Sussex, England, which he hated. He described the town as an "overblown gifte shoppe", and was always keen to get away.

Burra visited Spain on several occasions during the 1930s, his last visit forcibly cut short by the approaching Civil War. His paintings of Spain did not reflect the political situation, although their general mood grew progressively darker. The pained expression of this dancer's face, for example, is in marked contrast to his lighthearted view of the *Cuban Band* (also *c.* 1935). Some of the figures in the background of *Flamenco Dancers* have mask-like features and no eyes—indicative of a country losing its national soul. This trait, which is evident in many of his pictures, endeared him to the Surrealists.

CUBAN BAND (C. 1935)
Edward Burra (1905–76)

Mayor Gallery, London. Courtesy of The Bridgeman Art Library

Throughout his career, Burra was an inveterate traveler, always seeking out suitable subjects to paint. His personal preference was for raucous bars, where the music was boisterous, the drink was plentiful and the clientele rowdy enough to provide him with a colorful theme.

This painting was created shortly after Burra's first trip to the United States (1933–34). At this time he produced his pictures which are most closely associated with the Art Deco movement, not only because of their style but by virtue of the places in which he stayed. With a sense of adventure, he decided to explore Harlem and the Lower East Side of New York. There, he recorded the underbelly of the Jazz Age—the "cool dudes" lounging on the sidewalks, the sharp dressers parading in front of their friends, the hustle and bustle of people going about their business, and, most of all, the sweaty exuberance of the bars and the jazz clubs. Burra did not capture the scale of New York or the grandeur of its new buildings, in the way that both Lempicka and O'Keeffe did, but he provided an authentic record of life down on the streets.

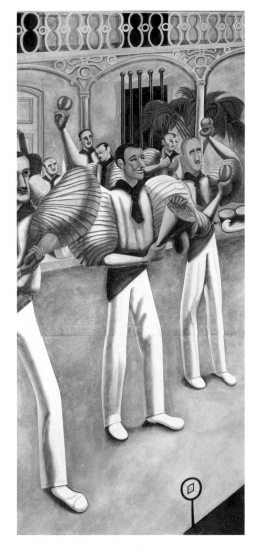

ANGELS OF PEACE (1948)
Jean Dupas (1882–1964)

Private Collection. Courtesy of The Bridgeman Art Library

Bordeaux-born Jean Dupas trained in the studios of Paul Alber Besnard (1849–1934) and Emile-Auguste Carolus-Duran (1878–1917). In 1910, he won the prestigious Prix de Rome, an award which signalled his ability as a conventional academic painter. Later he became a teacher at the Ecole des Beaux-Arts (1942–52).

In his early work, Dupas showed a preference for traditional Salon material—his first major painting was called *The Judgment of Paris* (1923)—although he gave it an unusual Modernist slant. The key influence appears to have come from Fernand Léger (1881–1955). But by the early 1920s, Dupas had developed a distinctive female type, which was to figure prominently in his work throughout his career. She had an impersonal, doll-like face and her limbs had a polished, tubular appearance, very much in the manner of Léger. Her body was stiffly articulated, rather like a puppet, and her hair would often flow out in stylized waves or ringlets. Almost without exception, she would also be accompanied by a small flock of doves, in the same way that his (rare) male figures would be attended by grayhounds. In most cases, the birds held no specific meaning, although in this ponderous allegory the doves and the olive branches were intended as symbols of peace.

LES PERRUCHES (THE PARAKEETS) (1925)
Jean Dupas (1882–1964)
Courtesy of Christie's Images

This is Dupas' most famous picture. It was specially commissioned for the 1925 Paris Exhibition, where it was displayed in one of the most important pavilions, Jacque-Emile Ruhlmann's (1879–1933) *Hôtel d'un Collectionneur.* The pavilion was modeled on a genuine mansion, which Ruhlmann had recently commissioned for himself, and it contained a wish list of fabulous items, created by the leading designers of the time.

Dupas had undertaken part of his artistic training in the studio of Emile-Auguste Carolus-Duran (1838–1917), a successful 19th-century Salon painter, and this left an indelible mark on the younger man's choice of subject matter. Many of his pictures have the air of classical mythologies, where carefree young women disport themselves in idyllic landscapes. Often, they have attributes—birds, flowers, unusual hats—which seem to hint at some symbolic meaning, but it is more likely that Dupas included them for decorative rather than symbolic effect. The artist employed the same basic composition in a wide variety of contexts. This charming scene, for example, is remarkably similar to a series of posters which he produced for London Transport in the 1930s. In these, Dupas' brief was simply to extol the beauties of the English countryside, and it is doubtful whether the meaning of *Les Perruches* is any more complex than that.

ARNOLD CONSTABLE (1928)
Jean Dupas (1882–1964)
Courtesy of E. T. Archive

The role of painting and fine art within the Art Deco movement has been the subject of some controversy. Several authorities have argued, for example, that the intellectual basis of fine art makes it wholly incompatible with a phenomenon that was essentially concerned with function and decoration, rather than ideas. Even if this objection can be laid aside, there is considerable disagreement over precisely which painters fall into the Art Deco camp. Although by no means a great artist, Jean Dupas' name is probably the one that is most frequently included. This is because he straddled a number of different fields, working with equal success as a painter, a poster designer, and a fashion illustrator.

The illustration shows a poster which Dupas designed for Arnold Constable, an American fashion firm. The female figure in the center is wearing the type of short dress that was all the rage at the time, but the image is perhaps most notable for its portrayal of past and future apparel. The former was reproduced faithfully from a 19th-century fashion plate, while the latter is notable for its extraordinary hat. Dupas may have been a frustrated milliner, because he enjoyed inventing elaborate headgear. Another example of fantastic millinery can be found worn by the girl in Dupas' 1925 *Les Perruches*.

ETOILE DU NORD (1927)
A.M. Cassandre (1901–68)

Haags Gemeentemuseum, Netherlands. Courtesy of AKG Photo

Adolphe Jean Marie Mouron, better known as Cassandre, was the most distinguished poster artist of the Art Deco era. He was born at Kharkov in the Ukraine, but moved to Paris in 1915. There, he studied to be a painter at the Ecole des Beaux-Arts and the Académie Julian. This training proved invaluable, as it enabled him to gain a full understanding of the many artistic theories—such as Cubism, Purism, Futurism, and Orphism—which were circulating in the French capital. He then allied these with the most up-to-date printing techniques, which he learned during his employment with Hachard et Compagnie, a firm of lithographic printers.

Cassandre designed his first poster in 1923, and won his first award in this field just two years later. In 1927, he formed a partnership, L'Alliance Graphique, with Charles Loupot (1892–1962) and Maurice Moyrand which operated until the latter's death in 1934. Two years later, Cassandre was accorded the honor of a solo-exhibition at the Museum of Modern Art in New York. He traveled to the US, working there from 1936 to 1939. On his return to France, he concentrated increasingly on designs for ballet and the theater. Cassandre's greatest posters were produced in the late 1920s. In these, he displayed his extraordinary gift for making complex images seem so simple to the viewer.

NORD EXPRESS (1927)
Cassandre (1901–68)
Courtesy of AKG Photo

Cassandre was particularly famous for his transport posters, most notably those advertising ocean liners and trains. In these, he adapted elements from a number of avant-garde artistic movements, which he had learned about while training as a painter. The most crucial influences came from Futurism and Purism, both of which celebrated the glories of modern machines and the excitement of speed.

In *Nord Express*, Cassandre conjures up an image of dynamic movement through the rapid convergence of differing perspectives. The telegraph lines on the right extend as far as the eye can see, and with diagonal lines of the locomotive hurtling towards them. The depiction of the train suggested by a few simple, geometric shapes—an obvious legacy of Cubism —also conveys a sense of the blurring that occurs at high speed, when the fine details of a moving object can no longer be seen.

Contemporaries hailed Cassandre for his inventive use of typography. In common with other designers, he liked to use functional, sans serif typefaces, accentuating their angularity by placing them squarely around the borders of the image. In *Nord Express*, he also drew attention to the company logo, by turning its edges red, where it intersected with the telegraph wires and the steam from the locomotive.

NEW STATENDAM TRAVEL POSTER (1928)
Cassandre (1901–68)
Courtesy of The Bridgeman Art Library

Cassandre produced several posters for cruise ships, which were widely copied by other designers. Most of Cassandre's posters focused on the scale of the vessel: in his advertisement for the French Line's cruise ship, the *Ile de France* (*c.* 1930), for example, he adopted a very low viewpoint, so that the hull of the ship loomed up like a skyscraper. He accentuated this by adding a minute flock of seagulls, silhouetted against the hull, to make the ship seem even larger. In this New Statendam Travel Poster, he zooms in very close, filling the entire picture space with a few details of the funnels. This also has the effect of distorting the scale of the ship, making it seem unnaturally large.

It is not hard to understand why designers placed such emphasis on the size of the luxury liners. The *Titanic* disaster may have been just a memory by 1928, but it was not yet a very distant one. Naturally shipping companies were anxious to reassure their clients that there would never be a repeat of the tragedy, because their liners were too large and too solidly built. It is also notable that Cassandre's poster places great emphasis on the word "comfort." For most passengers, the major attraction of the liners was the opportunity to share, if only for a little while, the luxurious lifestyle of the rich.

POSTER FOR THE FRENCH LINE (C. 1930)
Cassandre (1901–68)
Courtesy of The Bridgeman Art Library

This poster advertised the services of one of the most important Art Deco patrons, the Compagnie Générale Transatlantique, which was better known as either the CGT or the French Line. The company had only been in existence since 1912, and its beginnings could hardly have been less auspicious. The first ship it built, the *France*, embarked on its maiden voyage just five days after the loss of the *Titanic*. Worse still, the travel industry was hit hard by the First World War and subsequent economic problems. Despite these setbacks, the French Line survived and, by the 1920s, it had become one of Europe's leading travel companies.

The key to attracting new passengers was luxury. The *France* had been a genuine floating palace, with its interior modeled on the splendors of Versailles. In 1927, however, the CGT introduced a significant innovation. Its latest ship, the *Ile de France*, was just as opulent as its predecessors, but it was the first to be fitted out in a thoroughly modern style. As a result, the vessels of the French Line became an important showcase for the leading designers of the Art Deco movement. Every item of note, from the beds and the chairs down to the smallest item of cutlery, was fashioned in this style.

ANTI-NAZI POSTER (C. 1940)
Edward McKnight Kauffer (1890–1954)
Courtesy of AKG Photo

Edward McKnight Kauffer, American graphic designer and poster artist, was born in Great Falls, Montana. The son of a musician, Kauffer was working in a bookshop and attending evening classes in art, when a chance meeting changed his life. He made the acquaintance of Professor McKnight of Utah University, who was so impressed with the young man's artistic ambitions that he decided to help him. McKnight financed a trip to Europe and, out of gratitude, the youngster adopted his name. While en route for Paris, Kauffer stopped at Chicago, where he saw the Armory Show, the pioneering exhibition which introduced Modernist developments in the USA.

At the outbreak of the First World War, Kauffer moved to London, where he was soon influenced by the Vorticist movement. While under the spell of this dynamic, semi–abstract style, he produced his most famous poster, *Flight of Birds* (1919). With its blend of geometric elegance and sheer energy, this is generally accepted as one of the seminal images of Art Deco. Kauffer then divided his time between producing posters, for clients such as Shell and London Transport, and producing illustrations for the celebrated Nonesuch Press. He also wrote a book, *The Art of the Poster*. The pictured example is one of his later designs, produced for propaganda purposes during the Second World War.

ACTORS PREFER SHELL (1933)
Edward McKnight Kauffer (1890–1954)
Victoria and Albert Museum. Courtesy of The Bridgeman Art Library

The poster as an art form came of age during the Art Deco era. Until then it had been considered merely as adjunct to the recognized genres of fine art and book illustration. Posters in the late-19th and early-20th century often resembled preliminary sketches for paintings, stylized and easy to understand, usually accompanied by an obvious caption or title. Toulouse-Lautrec's posters for bars or theaters were typical of this trend, which was followed by a number of Art Deco designers. Painter and set designer Paul Colin's somewhat conservative poster for *La Revue Nègre* (1925), for example, was very much in this vein.

By the 1920s, however, the poster had become an invaluable commercial tool. Consumerism was on the rise, and companies were anxious to use the most direct means possible in order to attract customers. As a result, dynamic images and punchy slogans replaced the illustrative style of earlier posters. In this advertisement for Shell petrol, Kauffer conveyed his message using the vocabulary of Cubism. The basic components of acting—speech, gesture, sight, hearing—are assembled into a montage of semi-abstract forms and colors.

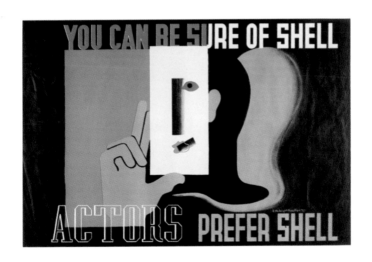

LA REVUE NÈGRE (1925)
Paul Colin (1892–1985)

Courtesy of AKG Photo

The decade of the 1920s may be viewed by some as the Art Deco years, but it was also the Jazz Age, the period when black culture gained an international reputation. In Paris, this was symbolized above all by the glittering career of Josephine Baker (1906–75). After performing as a dancer in a number of Harlem nightclubs, she arrived in Paris in 1925. Her first appearance, advertised here in Colin's poster, was in a show called *La Revue Nègre*, which was staged at the Champs-Elysées' Music-Hall. It took Paris by storm. The French had never seen black song-and-dance routines before, and they were entranced by Baker's blend of sassy charm and downright eroticism. She was swiftly dubbed "the Black Venus" and, after *La Revue Nègre* had finished its run, she was hired to perform at the Folies-Bergère. There, she took part in a show called *Un Vent du Folie* in which, accompanied by two cheetahs, she appeared on stage wearing nothing more than a skirt made out of imitation bananas.

Baker returned to New York in 1936, but Paris soon lured her back. She remained in France during the Second World War, serving in the French Women's Air Force and in the Resistance. Her bravery earned her both the *Croix de Guerre* and the Legion of Honour. She later became a Civil Rights campaigner in the US.

POSTER WITH BUGATTI RACING CAR (1926)
Ernst Deutsch-Dryden (1883–1938)
Courtesy of Christie's Images

Nothing epitomizes the glamor and modernity of the Art Deco period more succinctly than a fast car. Speed and elegance were worshipped in every quarter, and the streamlined appearance of cars often inspired designers in other fields. This particular make was pioneered by Ettore Bugatti, the son of the celebrated furniture designer. His first car was shown at the 1901 International Sports Exhibition in Milan, where it created a sensation. A Bugatti Type 13 won a notable victory at the Le Mans Grand Prix in 1911 and, within a few years, Ettore's cars appeared unbeatable. This poster, celebrating world championship success in 1926, was produced during the remarkable three-year period (1924–27), when a fleet of Bugattis won a staggering 1851 races. The pictured model is a Type 35, the most celebrated racing car of its time.

The creator of this image was Ernst Deutsch-Dryden (1883–1938). He studied under the Austrian artist Gustav Klimt, and began to specialize in poster design during the First World War. Subsequently, he turned his attention to fashion. He became art director of the German fashion magazine *Die Dame* in the 1920s, before moving to Hollywood and embarking on a career as a costume designer.

FOOTLIGHT PARADE (1933)
Busby Berkeley (1895–1976)
Courtesy of Pictorial Press Limited

In his stunning dance routines, Busby Berkeley translated the exuberance of Art Deco design on to the silver screen. Born William Berkeley Enos (his nickname derives from Amy Busby, a Broadway star from the turn of the century), he made his debut on stage at the age of five. He studied at a military school and served as a lieutenant during the First World War, before finding his true vocation on Broadway. In 1930, Samuel Goldwyn brought him to Hollywood, to choreograph some of the musical numbers for an Eddie Cantor film; Berkeley went on to produce his best work for Warner Brothers between 1933 and 1937.

Berkeley's routines exploited the taste for *trompe l'oeil* effects, which had been popular in Western art since the Renaissance. His performers did not so much dance as move into carefully arranged patterns—a blossoming flower, the American eagle, a gigantic neon violin. He set up a moving camera on a monorail, in order to capture these transformations, and horrified studio bosses by drilling holes in the ceiling, so that he could produce his distinctive overhead views (known in the business as "the Berkeley top shot"). In this fantasy sequence of 1933, rows of female bathers create a typically stylized design, against the backdrop of a rather showy Art Deco set.

GOLD DIGGERS OF 1935 (1935)
Busby Berkeley (1895–1976)
Courtesy of Pictorial Press Limited

After the phenomenal success of the *Gold Diggers of 1933* routine, Berkeley was asked to repeat the formula in a follow-up film two years later. This still from the film shows part of his dance routine for the Harry Warren song, "The Words are in my Heart." In characteristic fashion, Berkeley employed rows of identically dressed chorus girls to create kaleidoscopic effects. Here, the pianists form a geometric pattern which, at first glance, bears a passing resemblance to a piece of Art Deco jewelry.

Avery Hopwood's play, *The Gold Digger* (1919), spawned a series of films, which came to symbolize the dual nature of the Depression era—the contrast between the glamorous lifestyle of the rich and the plight of the unemployed. The rather slender plot, which revolved around a group of chorus girls chasing after wealthy husbands, gained an added poignancy when both the theater and film industry were hit by hard times. In *Gold Diggers of 1933*, for example, there was a painful irony about the opening number, "We're in the Money", which the singers performed in costumes made out of coins and dollar bills, just as their show was being closed down. After the 1935 film, the series lost its topical edge and the later sequels—*Gold Diggers of 1937*, and *Gold Diggers of Paris*—were less impressive.

A Pair of Side Chairs (1920s)
Jacques-Emile Ruhlmann (1879–1933)
Courtesy of Christie's Images

Jacques-Emile Ruhlmann is acknowledged as the finest of all the Art Deco furniture designers. His parents were from Alsace, but he was born in Paris. After completing his military service, he immediately began working for his father, who was a painting contractor. His lack of formal training was unusual for an aspiring designer, though it never hampered Ruhlmann's progress. In 1907, he took over the family business, following the death of his father, and this gave him the opportunity to experiment with his own designs.

In 1910, Ruhlmann made his first appearance in a public exhibition, showing a group of wallpaper designs at the Salon d'Automne. By 1913, he had switched his attention to furniture, displaying early examples of his work at the same venue. The outbreak of war prevented him from exhibiting again for several years, but by 1919 Ruhlmann's skills had matured considerably. He decided to change the emphasis of his father's business and went into partnership with Pierre Laurent, an old friend. It proved a wise move, as their association was to last until Ruhlmann's death. The firm expanded gradually, building up its reputation, though it was only at the Paris Exhibition of 1925 that it finally won the recognition it deserved.

AN OAK GAMES TABLE AND FOUR CHAIRS (C. 1927)
Jacques-Emile Ruhlmann (1879–1933)
Courtesy of Christie's Images

In 1925, Ruhlmann became a genuine celebrity, when his contribution to the Paris Exhibition attracted widespread attention. His display was housed in a pavilion which was known as the *Hôtel du Collectionneur* ("Residence for a Wealthy Art Collector"), designed by the architect Pierre Patout. Ruhlmann had enlisted the support of many leading designers, who assisted him with the scheme. Together, they devised a majestic suite of rooms, including a bedroom, bathroom, dining room, and boudoir, which drew enthusiastic crowds throughout the Exhibition.

The huge impact created by the *Hôtel du Collectionneur* resulted in a wealth of new commissions for Ruhlmann and his partner Laurent. One of the most prestigious of these concerned the luxurious ocean liner, *Ile de France*, which was in the process of being built. Ruhlmann was invited to create a Games Room for the new vessel, working in conjunction with a number of other prominent designers—among them, Jean Dunand, Jean Prouvé, and Jean Dupas. It was for this project that Ruhlmann produced the pictured chairs and table. The latter is made of oak and has a reversible top, while the chairs are upholstered in red hide and have moulded, tapering legs with gilt bronze mounts.

MACASSAR EBONY CHEVAL-MIRROR (C. 1920)
Jacques-Emile Ruhlmann (1879–1933)
Courtesy of Christie's Images

This is the type of furniture that gained Ruhlmann such a formidable reputation. Elegant and understated, it is one of his best-known creations. In essence, it appears incredibly basic—a simple vertical case, set on a tapering, pyramidal base. Its geometrical directness has since been cited as a prototype for the blossoming Art Deco style. As usual, though, Ruhlmann outstripped his competitors through his use of fine materials and his skill at orchestrating the decorative details of a piece. The chosen material in this instance is macassar ebony, although Ruhlmann is also known to have produced a near-identical version in burl amboina (a knotted Indonesian wood). The most eye-catching feature of this mirror is the delicate ivory inlay, which forms a scrollwork pattern on the base, an oval "beauty spot" at the top, and a network of slender, elongated lozenges on the swing-door. Records show that the mirror was exhibited at the Salon des Artistes Décorateurs in 1922, which dates the original design to around 1920.

A BURL AMBOINA SIDEBOARD (C. 1930)
Jacques-Emile Ruhlmann (1879–1933)

Courtesy of Christie's Images

Throughout his career, Ruhlmann took great pride in using the rarest and most expensive materials for his furniture. Along with amboina, which is a mottled Indonesian wood, he enjoyed working with a range of exotic woods—amaranth, macassar ebony, rosewood, Cuban mahogany—inlaying them with ivory, tortoise shell or horn. Amboina was a particular favourite, because it had an attractive knotty pattern (the burl), which could help produce a rich graining effect on the finished piece. Certainly, the proportions of this sideboard are beautifully balanced. The curved central section is flanked by two cabinets and topped by a shaped slab of veined marble. Inside, the cupboards are made of oak.

The piece cannot be dated with certainty, but it must date from after 1925, when Ruhlmann began to add metal mounts to his furniture. The silver-plated lock used here is much less conspicuous than the large, octagonal mount which he used on one of his late cabinets, but the geometric design may have been less to his liking, which is possibly why he changed his style. The lock on this sideboard bears the signature of J. Martel: the brothers Joel and Jan Martel were both sculptors and designers. They often worked together, producing Cubist-inspired sculpture in concrete, stone or metal.

ROSEWOOD AND GILT BRONZE DAY-BED (1920s)
Jacques-Emile Ruhlmann (1879–1933)
Courtesy of Christie's Images

This day-bed is a model known as "Ducharnebronz". It is made of Brazilian rosewood, though the armrests and the back are edged with gilded bronze. At the front, the bed rests on two fluted, cylindrical feet, while at the rear there is a larger support, which once again is made of gilded bronze. The neat, geometric shape of the object is emphasised by the rectangular cushions and cylindrical bolsters.

Although he is perhaps most famous for his exquisitely veneered cabinets, sideboards and other such items, Ruhlmann was above all the master ensemblier of his time; that is to say, he created entire interiors: from the tiniest ashtray to a king-size bed. In following this path, Ruhlmann developed enormous versatility, which enabled him to turn his hand to the design of any object, and also a phenomenal eye for detail. He appeared to find it difficult to manifest this skill in his sketches; since he never undertook a formal apprenticeship he employed a team of skilled draughtsmen, who were able to transform his ideas into tangible reality. In keeping with his attitude concerning all aspects of his craft, Ruhlmann was determined that only the most skilful workmen should be on his payroll, willingly paying them more than the normal rate for their services.

ROSEWOOD CABINET (1933)
Jacques-Emile Ruhlmann (1879–1933)
Courtesy of Christie's Images

This sumptuous cabinet, made of Brazilian rosewood, was designed by Ruhlmann in the last year of his life. It indicates just how well the master *ébéniste* was able to adapt to meet the demands of a changing market. For much of his career, Ruhlmann had been lukewarm about the notion of using unconventional materials, but he did eventually become accustomed to the idea of adding metal mounts on his work. In this instance, the plated-bronze lockplate is by Foucault, with whom he had already collaborated on several occasions. Foucault's tiptoeing nude figure bears little resemblance to the normal Art Deco canon of female beauty. Instead, she is rather more akin to a decorative nymph from the rococo era, the period which Ruhlmann so admired.

The designer's determination to push himself into new ventures remained firm until the end. One of his final commissions was to provide the décor for a play at the Comédie Française. Ruhlmann had never tackled this kind of job before, but he accepted the challenge and designed an ingenious set, which incorporated several pieces of his furniture. Within a few months he was dead, and his business died with him. A year later, Madame Ruhlmann organized a retrospective exhibition of his work, to demonstrate what a great talent France had lost.

OAK MIRROR
Carlo Bugatti (1856–1940)
Courtesy of Christie's Images

Carlo Bugatti was a maverick designer, whose work cannot easily be categorized in any single genre. Born in Milan, the son of a sculptor, Carlo's initial ambition was to become an architect. By 1880, however, he had switched his attention to furniture and in 1888 he opened his own workshop in Milan. He began displaying his designs at exhibitions in Italy, France, and England. His originality was soon recognized and he won several awards, among them a silver medal at the Paris Exhibition of 1900 and a Diploma of Honour at the Turin Exhibition of 1902.

Bugatti moved to Paris in 1904, where he divided his time between painting and furniture design. He also began to design silver, displaying the results at the Galérie Hébrard. Before the First World War, Bugatti exhibited at the Salon des Artistes Décorateurs, where many of the future Art Deco designers had an opportunity to study his work at close quarters. His designs won high praise in a number of prestigious journals, including *Kunst und Kunsthandwerk* and *Art et Décoration*, but Bugatti remained slightly suspicious of such plaudits, preferring to glory in his chosen role as an isolated eccentric. His son, Ettore, later made the family name synonymous with fast racing cars, as can be seen in Ernst Deutsch-Dryden's *Poster with Bugatti Racing Car* (1926).

OAK CHEST OF DRAWERS (C. 1900–10)
Carlo Bugatti (1856–1940)
Courtesy of Christie's Images

This striking chest offers a fine example of Bugatti's unique style. It is inlaid with a variety of different woods, hammered brass, and bone. These form a number of eye-catching patterns, ranging from traditional lozenge and chequer-board motifs to stylized flowers and dragonflies. The mirror is flanked by two vitrines, and the rectangular body includes three drawers and a drop-flap.

Bugatti's work does not conform neatly with any of the recognized styles of design. He is most closely associated with the *Stile Liberty*, the Italian equivalent of the Art Nouveau movement, largely on account of his use of zoomorphic forms (at the Turin Exhibition, for example, he produced an entire suite of furniture based on the shape of a snail's shell). On the other hand, he was also an important source of inspiration for Art Deco designers. In particular, they admired the exotic flavor of much his work, his use of unconventional materials and his readiness to combine very different stylistic elements in one piece of work. In this piece, for example, a curvilinear Art Nouveau mirror is placed in a Moorish-inspired setting. Small wonder that one critic remarked that he reminded him more of H. Rider Haggard (the author of *King Solomon's Mines*), than of any other designer.

DOUBLE BED (C. 1925)
Maurice Dufrène (1876–1955)
Courtesy of Christie's Images

Maurice Dufrène was a leading cabinet-maker and interior designer, who successfully bridged the transition from Art Nouveau to Art Deco. He began by studying philosophy, but switched to a design course at the Ecole des Arts Décoratifs. After graduating, he worked for a time in a modern print house, before joining La Maison Moderne, Meier-Graefe's showcase for the latest developments in interior design. When this closed in 1903, Dufrène became a founder member of the Salon des Artistes Décorateurs. For many years, this was to be the main forum for his work. Dufrène is best remembered for his links with La Maîtrise, the influential design studio, which sold its wares at Paris's Galeries Lafayette. He was the founding director of this studio, using it to promote his own views on modern furniture. In these, he was firmly in line with conventional Art Deco thinking, believing that cheap, mass-produced furniture was a positive development, but that this should in no way compromise either the quality of the design or the comfort of the finished product. "In what way is a machine less important than a tool?" he enquired. "Where does the tool end and the machine begin? Isn't a planer a small machine?"

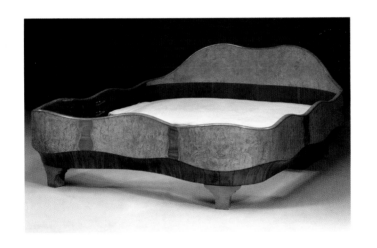

SALON SUITE (C. 1925)
Maurice Dufrène (1876–1955)
Courtesy of Christie's Images

These striking giltwood seats, with matching tapestry upholstery, are part of a five-piece Salon suite. The full ensemble consists of a canapé, two bergères (only one illustrated), a foot stool and a window seat. The exotic tapestry design was produced at the Beauvais works. It may represent a scene from the famous French novel, *Paul et Virginie*, which was partially set in Mauritius.

Tapestry underwent something of a revival during the Art Deco era. Its use in screens and wall coverings had become old-fashioned, particularly as so many of the designs were nothing more than reproductions of paintings. This attitude changed during the 1920s and 1930s. The pioneering figure was Jean Lurçat (1892–1966), who introduced bold, geometric patterns in his work for Aubusson. Dufrène's suite predates this development but, together with André Mare and Marianne Clouzot, he did much to encourage the use of Modernist designs on his furniture. At La Maîtrise, he engaged a tapestry specialist, Jean Beaumont, to produce designs for the shop Galéries Lafayette. Beaumont went on to win his most impressive commission in 1932, when he was asked to design curtains for the *Normandie*, one of the grandest of the luxury liners.

OAK AND WROUGHT-IRON DINING TABLE (c. 1938)
Gilbert Poillerat (b. 1902)
Courtesy of Christie's Images

The Art Deco years witnessed a great revival in the field of decorative metalwork. The clean lines and plain materials of Modernist architecture offered exciting new opportunities for designers in this field. Some of these openings were the result of new technology—for instance lift cages and electric light fittings demanded a whole new approach to design—but there was also a call for more traditional metalwork items, such as stairways and balustrades.

Gilbert Poillerat was one of a cluster of young French designers who made their mark in this field. He studied initially at the Ecole Boulle, and then spent the early years of his career working for Edgar Brandt, the leading metalworker of the day. In the late 1920s, Poillerat joined the construction firm of Baudet, Donon, and Roussel, mainly producing decorative grilles, panels, and screens. Poillerat's most prestigious work in this vein came in the following decade, when he was commissioned to design the bronze doors for the *Normandie*'s swimming pool (1935). In the intervening period, he had begun designing jewelry for the fashion business, producing some of his most imaginative pieces for a couturier named Jacques Heim. The finesse and intricate detail that were considered necessary in this type of work influenced Poillerat's other designs of the period; the delicate ornamentation of this table is a good example of his skill.

WROUGHT-IRON FIRE SCREEN (C. 1930)
Edgar Brandt (1880–1960)
Courtesy of Christie's Images

Edgar Brandt was the leading metalworker of the age. After training under Emile Robert, he designed jewelry for a time, before setting up his own studio in 1919. In the same year, he also began exhibiting at the Salon des Artistes Décorateurs and the Salon d'Automne. Soon, he was being entrusted with major decorative schemes. In 1921, he was commissioned to provide parts of the official war memorial at Verdun, and he later carried out similar work for the Tomb of the Unknown Soldier in Paris.

Brandt's reputation was forged at the 1925 Exhibition, both through the designs on show in his own pavilion, and through the wrought-iron doors and light fittings he produced for other exhibitors. His success enabled him to open up two overseas showrooms, in London and New York. The latter, which traded under the name of Ferrobrandt, brought him lucrative commissions for the Cheney Building and the Montreal Chamber of Commerce, while his English connection led him to provide decorations for Selfridges department store in London. The wrought-iron fire screen pictured highlights the delicacy of Brandt's work, which was seen to its best advantage on screens, panels, and gates.

WROUGHT-IRON AND MARBLE TABLE (1920s)
Raymond Subes (1893–1970)

Courtesy of Christie's Images

Raymond Subes was one of the most prolific and sought-after designers of the Art Deco era, but his work is hard to assess, since much of it forms an anonymous part of larger architectural commissions. He studied at both the Ecole Boulle and the Ecole National Supérieure des Arts Décoratifs, where he specialized in metallurgy. He then undertook an apprenticeship in the studio of Emile Robert, who had pioneered the revival of metalwork in the 19th century.

Subes exhibited tables such as this at the two Salons that focused on the decorative arts (the Salon des Artistes Décorateurs and the Salon d'Automne), but the bulk of his work was produced for the construction company Borderel et Robert, of which he was a director. For the company, he produced decorative grilles, doors, balustrades, and panels; these varied commissions related to a diverse assortment of projects, ranging from hotels, offices, and exhibition halls to churches and cemeteries. His most prestigious commissions included orders for wrought-iron gates at the Musée Permanent des Colonies (Colonial Museum), Paris, and the Oceanographical Museum in Biarritz; as well as an ornate bronze door for the dining-room in the ill-fated liner *Normandie*.

LACQUERED DRESSING TABLE (C. 1930)
Paul Follot (1877–1941)
Courtesy of Christie's Images

Paul Follot enjoyed a distinguished career as an interior designer, adapting to a succession of different styles throughout his life. He was the son of a notable wallpaper designer and trained under Eugène Grasset, best known today for his Art Nouveau posters. Follot's beginnings were highly eclectic. His first published designs were Neo-Gothic and he displayed an early interest in sculpture, but he made his mark producing Art Nouveau jewelry and textiles for La Maison Moderne. As he turned his attention towards furniture, his style became more unusual and some of his prewar pieces have been hailed as pioneering masterpieces of Art Deco design. These won him some prestigious appointments in the 1920s: in 1923, he was made director of the Atelier Pomone, which marketed its wares at Le Bon Marché, a department store; five years later, he moved to the Paris branch of Waring & Gillow, a famous British firm.

In common with other French designers, Follot retained a marked traditional element in his work, indicated by his preference for the light woods and rounded forms that had been popular since the 18th century. His use of materials, however, was highly adventurous. In this lacquered dressing table, for example, the cylindrical steel pedestals and the alabaster scrollwork lampshades lend a very modern flavor to an otherwise traditional piece.

MAPLE-WOOD DESK (C. 1925)
attributed to Dominique (1922–70)
Courtesy of Christie's Images

Dominique was a prolific, highly regarded decorating firm, which enjoyed its greatest success during the Art Deco years. The firm's founder was André Domin (1883–1962), a self-taught artist from Caen. In 1922, he went into partnership with Marcel Genevrière (1885–?), an accomplished architect. Together, they designed a broad range of furniture, textiles, and wrought-iron decoration. Their reputation was sealed after two early commissions earned them high praise. These were decorations at the home of Jean Puiforcat (1897–1945), the silversmith, and the refurbishments at the Houbigant perfume factory, both commissioned in 1923.

The firm gained further plaudits for its displays at the 1925 Paris Exhibition, where it contributed to the lounge in the Ambassade Française. Capitalizing on these achievements, Domin joined forces with four other designers to form "Les Cinq". These "newcomers" were already established figures in their respective fields: Jean Puiforcat; Raymond Templier (1891–1968), a distinguished member of a family of jewelers; Pierre Chareau (1883–1950), an architect and furniture designer; and Pierre Legrain (1887–1929), a bookbinder and interior decorator. This formidable group exhibited their wares together over the next few years, winning a number of lucrative commissions. The most notable of these concerned the refurbishment of a hotel in Havana, and the creation of a luxury suite of apartments in the ocean liner *Normandie*.

A Set of Macassar Ebony Armchairs (1920s)
Paul Kiss
Courtesy of Christie's Images

This illustration shows part of a set of six chairs, attributed to the Romanian artist, Paul Kiss. He carved out a niche for himself with his unusual designs in wrought iron and other forms of metalwork. These were normally applied to consoles, grilles, large torchères, or substantial pieces of furniture. Seats of this kind are less typical of his work, although the ingenious metal trimmings have a familiar look. Kiss produced a number of lampstands with extended, leaf-shaped segments, which are reminiscent of the scrolling back-panels on these armchairs. The panels are held in place by hammered brass borders and a rigid top rail, which give the seats a decidedly uncomfortable appearance.

Born in Balafalva, Romania, Kiss spent a nomadic existence in Hungary and Germany, before settling in France. He collaborated for a time with Edgar Brandt, and the latter's designs had a profound effect on his work. Kiss exhibited regularly at the principal outlets for applied art—the Salon des Artistes Décorateurs, the Salon d'Automne, and the Salon des Artistes Français—and he opened his own showroom in Paris. This attracted many commissions, particularly after the artist's impressive display at the 1925 Exhibition.

THREE ITEMS FROM A FIVE-PIECE BENTWOOD SUITE (EARLY 1900s)
Josef Maria Olbrich (1867–1908)

Courtesy of Christie's Images

Art Deco taste was highly eclectic, drawing its inspiration from a diverse collection of styles and movements. One of its primary sources can be found in the Vienna Secession, which was founded in 1897 by Gustav Klimt. This group's interests ranged from painting to the applied arts, and its most immediate impact was on the development of *Jugendstil* (the Germanic equivalent of Art Nouveau). In the longer term, however, the Secession's concern with logic, geometry, and function was also important for the emerging Art Deco style.

Josef Maria Olbrich was one of the key figures of the Vienna Secession. Born in Silesia, the son of a baker, his principal interest was in architecture. He designed the venue for the group's second exhibition (1898), together with a range of buildings and interiors for another collective, the Darmstadt Artists' Colony. As a graphic artist, Olbrich was responsible for many illustrations in *Ver Sacrum*, the Secession's official magazine. In addition, he produced designs for furniture, wallpaper, lighting, and cutlery. These were conceived as part of his interior schemes, rather than as individual pieces. His best-known furniture, for example, was produced for the Villa Stift (1899) and the Opel Worker's House (1908). The furniture pictured here is made of polished wood with a mahogany stain and it is upholstered in a woven flower pattern. The feet have square-section bronze sabots.

AN ENGLISH THREE-PIECE SUITE (1920s)
Anon
Courtesy of Christie's Images

In Europe, Art Deco was primarily a French phenomenon and there is considerable disagreement about the extent of its influence in other countries. The prevailing view is that the British were still firmly attached to the Arts and Crafts Movement, and reacted very slowly to the new trend. This would appear to be borne out by the pictured suite, which is rather a tame version of Parisian models, notable only for its attractive cloud-shaped arms.

The most talented designer to come from Great Britain was an Irishwoman, Eileen Gray (1878–1976), who produced superb lacquer-work and tubular furniture. In England itself, there were only sporadic signs of progress. Sir Ambrose Heal (1872–1959) began to design Modernist furniture after the 1925 Exhibition, as did Sir Edward Brantwood Maufe (1883–1974), who is, however, probably better remembered as the architect of Guildford Cathedral. The most promising development in Britain was the creation of the Omega Workshops, founded in 1913 by Roger Fry (1866–1934) and clearly modelled on the Wiener Werkstätte in Vienna. The workshops attracted a formidable array of talent—among others, Duncan Grant (1885–1978), Vanessa Bell (1879–1961), Nina Hamnett (1890–1956) and Edward McKnight Kauffer (1890–1954)—but the organisation was chaotic and there were claims of amateurism, which led to the workshops' closure in 1920.

OAK CUPBOARD (1930s)
André-Léon Arbus (1903–69)

Courtesy of Christie's Images

André-Léon Arbus faced a dilemma that was shared by many designers of his generation. He came from a highly traditional background—both his father and grandfather had been cabinet-makers—and he struggled to come to terms with the latest Modernist developments, with their emphasis on functionalism and mass-production.

Arbus began by studying law, before deciding to join the family business. He began showing his work frequently, both at the Paris Salon and at international exhibitions. Through these, he won a number of awards, such as the Prix Blumenthal (1935). His designs gained exposure through his Parisian gallery, L'Epoque, which he opened in 1930.

Much of Arbus's furniture displayed the sleek lines that were so adored by the Modernists, but he contrasted these with rich materials and metal adornments. His upholstery would often have an exotic flavor, while his wardrobes and dressers were decorated with elaborate bronze mounts. In the pictured example, the severe angularity of the cupboard is offset by its ornate handle, which takes the form of a Gorgon's head, its hair writhing with snakes. This combination of the old and the new was much admired by critics. As one of them declared, "Arbus feels that the French home does not need to offer a faithful reflection of this century of iron and reinforced concrete. Instead, it should compensate for it."

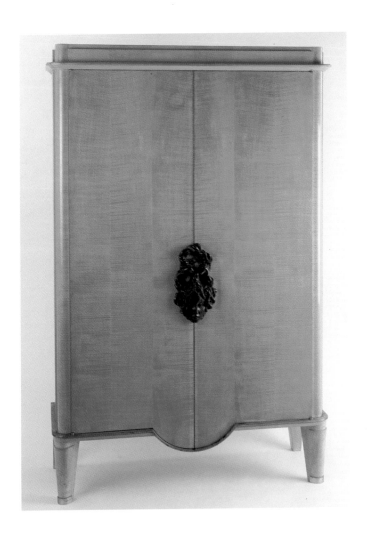

A PAIR OF WALNUT BEDSIDE CABINETS (LATE 1920S)
attributed to Eric Bagge (1890–1978)

Courtesy of Christie's Images

The attribution for these cabinets is based on a maker's plaque, which confirms that the pieces were originally retailed by Mercier Frères, a Parisian store where Eric Bagge sold much of his work. The cabinets themselves are set on chamfered plinths and their elegant, lotus-shaped design was inspired by the craze for Egyptian styles, which is evident in so many Art Deco buildings. This connection lends further weight to the attribution, since Bagge certainly regarded architecture as being his primary sphere of activity.

Bagge is one of the lesser-known figures in the Art Deco movement. After training as an architect, he was employed as lecturer at the Ecole des Arts Appliqués. He designed a number of shops in Paris—among them the boutiques of jeweler Henri Dubret, and the furriers Guélis Frères—along with several pavilions at international exhibitions. Initially, his style was quite opulent, although he later introduced a more stylized, geometric element into his designs, most notably in the living room which he created for the *Ile de France*. When designing furniture, Bagge often collaborated with Bernard Huguet and employed the firm of G. & J. Dennery to execute the work.

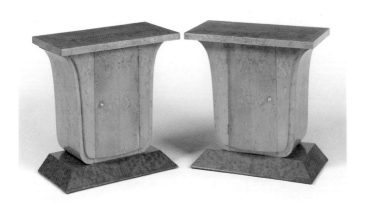

Swivel Chair and Stool (1980s)
Tom Dixon
Courtesy of Christie's Images

Tom Dixon appears to have drawn some of his inspiration for these pieces from the Art Deco taste for exotic decoration and unusual materials. The swivel chair is made out of welded sheet steel, decorated with black lacquer and blue upholstery. It is set on an arresting, geometric base, which consists of an arched panel, a pyramidal column and four triangular feet—all prominent features of Art Deco furniture created in the 1920s and 1930s. The stool, which is made of cast iron and steel, has an even more unconventional base. Its steel legs are attached to converted gas junctions.

In a similar vein, Dixon created a chair in 1986–87, which was composed of cast iron and "found" objects. The back support, for example, was comprised of assorted railings, rescued from demolition sites. At the same period, he also produced another remarkable chair, composed of S-shaped loops of metal, attached to a steel and aluminium base. The exclusive nature of Dixon's work is very different from the Art Deco obsession with mass-production; the chair that featured found objects was, for obvious reasons, a one-off creation, and much of his furniture is executed only in limited batches. Even so, the sheer panache of his work probably owes something to the masterpieces of Subes and Brandt or the exotica of Bugatti.

HAND-KNOTTED WOOLLEN CARPET (C. 1929)
Edward McKnight Kauffer (1890–1954)

Courtesy of Christie's Images

Kauffer is known mainly for his posters and other graphic work but, in the late 1920s and early 1930s, he also produced a number of textile designs. This appears to have come about as a result of his relationship with Marion Dorn (1899–1964). The pair became drawn to each other in the early 1920s, partially because they were both expatriate Americans. Born in San Francisco, Dorn was educated at Stamford University and traveled to Europe in 1923. Soon, she began living with Kauffer, although they were not actually married until 1950.

In the late 1920s, Dorn and Kauffer began collaborating on textile designs. Their initial efforts were made for batik fabrics, although they soon switched their attention to woven carpets. In 1929, they staged a major exhibition at the Arthur Tooth Gallery, displaying the designs that they had created for the Wilton Royal Carpet Factory. This geometric design, which has some affinities with constructivism, may have been one of the items on show. Kauffer soon returned to graphic art, but Dorn founded her own firm in 1934 and became a leading figure in this field. She was later commissioned to produce carpeting for both the Savoy and Claridges, as well as the liners *Orion* and *Queen Mary*.

A Mahogany and Brass Newspaper Rack (c. 1910)
Gustave Serrurier-Bovy (1858–1910)
Courtesy of Christie's Images

This interesting piece illustrates the fluid nature of artistic boundaries. Serrurier's main associations were with Art Nouveau and the English Arts and Crafts Movement; he died before the Art Deco bandwagon was truly underway. Nevertheless, his later works demonstrate just how early the taste for strict geometric shapes began to emerge.

Gustave Serrurier was born in Liège, the son of a cabinet-maker. He trained as an architect and was working in this field, when he traveled to England in 1884. There he met and married Maria Bovy, adopting her surname. Together, they opened a shop in Liège, selling Liberty fabrics and wallpaper. Serrurier was still designing and in 1894 he exhibited some furniture at La Libre Esthétique. Its style was strange enough to prompt one critic to describe it as "rustico-gothico-britannique." This did not deter Serrurier from contributing to further exhibitions, although his interest in the flowing, curvilinear forms of Art Nouveau became more apparent. By 1900, business was prospering on all fronts: his shop, L'Art dans l'Habitation, was doing well, he was running a factory in Liège; and his designs were winning increasing respect. In his final years, however, his style became more rectilinear, providing an intriguing foretaste of Art Deco.

PERFUME, A GILT AND LACQUER PANEL
(C. 1925)
Jean Dunand (1887–1942)

Courtesy of Christie's Images

Jean Dunand was a Swiss designer who trained as a sculptor; many of his early designs were for beaten metalware. In 1909, however, he changed direction, after seeing the lacquer designs produced by oriental craftsmen in Paris. By 1912, he had made contact with the Japanese master, Sugawara, learning traditional techniques from him. These methods were extremely slow and painstaking, consisting of no fewer than 22 separate stages. Dunand followed these dutifully, but also experimented tirelessly in the hope of creating new effects. His greatest success came with the use of crushed eggshell, which gave him a new shade of white—unobtainable through vegetable dyes—and also enabled him to create a variety of different textures.

Dunand's lacquerware proved extremely popular and his studio expanded rapidly. Many of his employees were from Indochina, and this had a telling impact on his work. There is a pronounced oriental influence, for example, in the design of this lavish panel. The vogue for fine lacquerware was comparatively short-lived. It was defeated by the demands of mass production, being gradually superseded by japanning—a much cheaper, synthetic process. Dunand's work continued to attract the costlier end of the market, however, and he won a series of lucrative commissions from the luxury liners.

WALL PLAQUE (PRE-1930)
Clarice Cliff (1899–1972)
Courtesy of Christie's Images

Clarice Cliff was the most inventive and original ceramicist in the Art Deco movement. She was born at Tunstall, Staffordshire, and, at the age of 13, began an apprenticeship as an enameler in a local pottery firm. In 1918, she was hired as an engraver by A. J. Wilkinson Ltd., a branch of the Royal Staffordshire Pottery. Here, Cliff enjoyed a close relationship with the managing director, eventually marrying him in 1941. He gave her the opportunity to develop her unique talents at the Newport Pottery, which Wilkinson's had taken over. In this environment, Cliff began to produce the jazzy, geometric designs for which she was to become famous.

This wall plaque is an unusual example of Cliff's work. Human figures rarely featured in her work, but this design depicts a Russian couple in extravagant peasant costume, dancing in front of a fairy-tale castle and snow-capped mountains. They were probably inspired by Diaghilev's ballets, which are known to have made a great impression on the artist. Cliff painted the scene on a *Latona* ground—a creamy, matte glaze, which she had developed herself as an alternative to Wilkinson's shinier glazes. She produced only a few of these plaques, which were usually made as special presents for the girls employed in her workshop.

LUGANO COFFEE POT, CUP AND SAUCER (1930)
Clarice Cliff (1899–1972)
Courtesy of Christie's Images

These items come from Clarice Cliff's *Bizarre* brand of tableware. She chose the unusual name herself, when her designs were first marketed in 1928, hoping that it would help to attract attention to them. The ploy was successful, for the public was soon clamoring for her work, and the Newport studio expanded rapidly. The designs consisted principally of stark, geometric shapes, executed in bold colors, although some compositions were based on stylized flowers or landscapes. The shapes of the objects themselves were also unusual. Plates might be square or hexagonal, for instance, and the triangular handles on the illustrated pieces are equally striking.

The pictured items are from the *Appliqué* range, which Cliff introduced in 1930. Each piece featured extensive decoration and, because of the amount of labor involved, the retail price was rather high. The images in the series were borrowed from the designs of a French artist, Edouard Benedictus (1878–1930). The earliest patterns were *Appliqué Lucerne*, which featured a castle, and *Appliqué Lugano* (pictured), which depicted a watermill, but at least eight other designs were also produced. The *Appliqué* range does not appear to have been particularly successful, perhaps on account of the price, but it remained available until 1933.

SILVER TEA SERVICE (C. 1927–28)
Josef Hoffmann (1870–1956)

Courtesy of Christie's Images

It is a popular misconception that Art Deco styles were confined to the 1920s and 1930s. In fact, the roots of the movement were well developed before the outbreak of the First World War. In the applied arts, some of the foundations were laid by an art-workers co-operative known as the Wiener Werkstätte, which was founded in 1903. This in turn was an offshoot of the Vienna Secession, a dissident group formed in 1897 by Gustav Klimt (1862–1918). One of its members was the designer Josef Hoffmann who, together with Koloman Moser, became the driving force behind the Workshops. His work ranged from textiles and furniture to metalwork and jewelry. Initially, he worked in a severe, rectilinear style, which had a profound influence on later Art Deco designers.

This four-piece tea service bears the Wiener Werkstätte stamp and is signed with Hoffmann's monogram. It is made from hammered silver with teak handles and finials. Its most distinctively Art Deco features are the squat, cylindrical feet that support the three containers. At almost any other period, these would have been slender and tapering. In addition, the ribbed decoration includes a subtle zigzag pattern, one of the most common Art Deco motifs.

SILVER TEA AND COFFEE SERVICE (C. 1934–39)
H. G. Murphy (?–1939)
Courtesy of Christie's Images

By and large, English silversmiths were far more conservative than their French counterparts during this period, but there were a few notable exceptions. Throughout the 1930s, H. G. Murphy displayed a pronounced liking for the geometric motifs and radical stylisations of Art Deco. This did not always go down well in an environment where the Worshipful Company of Goldsmiths encouraged craftsmen to concentrate on practical items, such as cutlery, and produce only the occasional unusual piece for exhibition purposes. Accordingly, when Murphy proceeded to display a set of silver boxes with unusual finials (representing, among other things, a beehive and a stylized cascade), the clerk of the company dismissed them as "Murphy trying to outdo the Germans in art and decoration and going modern."

This jazzy six-piece service is one of Murphy's crowning achievements. It comprises two coffee pots, a teapot, a milk jug, a sugar bowl, and a spoon. The drum-shaped bodies of the vessels provide an engaging contrast with the geometric elements—the triangular spouts, the wedge-shaped rosewood handles, and the angular finials. This was apparently one of Murphy's final designs. One of the coffee pots was unfinished at the time of his death in 1939, and was assembled and hallmarked posthumously.

SOUP TUREEN (C. 1930)
Jean Puiforcat (1897–1945)
Courtesy of Christie's Images

Jean Puiforcat was the premier silversmith of the Art Deco period. He learnt his craft in the studio of his father, who in turn came from a long line of goldsmiths; Jean also received lessons in sculpture from Louis Lejeune. Puiforcat began exhibiting his work in 1922, and was soon winning plaudits throughout the design world. As a result of his growing reputation, he was co-opted onto a range of exhibition committees, among them the Paris shows of 1925 and 1937. He was also one of the original members of the Union des Artists Modernes, which was founded in 1930 to help promote the cause of Modernism in the industrial arts.

Throughout his career, Puiforcat was best known for his tea sets, food vessels, and cutlery. From the outset, he kept ornamental detail to a minimum, preferring to let the high quality of the materials create its own impact. Early items often featured handles of ivory or jade but, as his talent matured, Puiforcat decided that even these details were too distracting. His work from the 1930s was sleek and geometric, sometimes almost futuristic in appearance. This elegant tureen is made of white metal and is parcel gilt (that is, "partially gilded").

SILVER DINNER SERVICE (1935)
Jean Puiforcat (1897–1945)

Courtesy of Christie's Images

Puiforcat was a founder member of the Union des Artistes Modernes, which took as its motto, *"le beau dans l'utile"* ("the beauty in usefulness"). Few designers pursued this ideal with greater dedication than this Frenchman. His family had been goldsmiths for generations, but Puiforcat made a radical departure from the style traditionally associated with his craft. In place of the opulent ornamentation that wealthy clients frequently demanded, he began to use severe, geometric stylisations. The roots of this style can be found in the work of Josef Hoffmann and the Wiener Werkstätte, although some critics preferred to link it to Cubism. Puiforcat was cautious about such comparisons. "For me, all that I have made is not definitively modern," he wrote. "If there is one desire I have for my work, it is not to be at the mercy of a formula, but to arrive at that which I feel and can freely express."

This 160-piece dinner service was produced as part of one of Puiforcat's most prestigious commissions. It was specifically designed for use on board the *Normandie*, the luxury liner launched in 1934. The boat was intended to be the most spectacular of the "floating palaces" in operation, and its interior and fittings were created by many leading Art Deco designers.

COCKTAIL SHAKER AND SMOKING SET (1920s)
Anon
Courtesy of Christie's Images

These two items combine the contemporary passion for the latest modes of transport with two of the period's most fashionable vices—drinking and smoking. The item above is a cocktail shaker, designed in the form of a zeppelin. The electroplate body can be taken apart to reveal a set of spoons and beakers, a lemon squeezer, a spirit flask, a corkscrew, and a measure. Not surprisingly, the shaker was made in Germany, where zeppelins were regarded as the most stylish form of transport, until the disastrous flight of the *Hindenburg* in 1937, which ended with the airship bursting into flames. Cocktails were the fashionable drinks of the day, spawning a host of Art Deco accessories and explanatory books. One of the latter informed enthusiasts that the name derived from Coctel, an ancient Mexican princess. It also exhorted drinkers to "shake the shaker as hard as you can: you are trying to wake it up, not send it to sleep."

The chrome smoking set is in the form of the latest propeller plane. Once again, its modest dimensions conceal a fine array of accessories: a tobacco holder, a cigar-cutter, two cigarette cases, and three ashtrays.

WROUGHT-IRON STANDARD LAMP (1920s)
Katona and Muller

Courtesy of Christie's Images

This is a typical example of the new style of standard lamp, which became popular in the 1920s. The type of lamp emerged to meet the growing demand for indirect lighting: that which reflected the glare of the bulb up towards the ceiling. Designs of this kind usually called for a partnership between metalworkers and glassmakers, since wrought-iron bases were generally more common than wooden ones. This Katona stand takes the form of an openwork column, with leaf-and-berry motifs and scrolling underneath the lamp.

The lampshade bears the signature *Muller Frères*. This refers to a long-established family of designers, who operated from a studio in Nancy. It was a sizable family, consisting of no fewer than nine brothers, five of whom had been apprenticed to the celebrated Emile Gallé (1846–1904). Another of the brothers and a sister learned their trade at the St Louis glassworks, before having to flee at the outbreak of the Franco-Prussian War (1870–71). The Mullers set up their own studio in *c.* 1895 and were still working during the Art Deco era. Initially they specialized in birds and floral subjects, but they adapted well to the more abstract requirements of the 1920s designers.

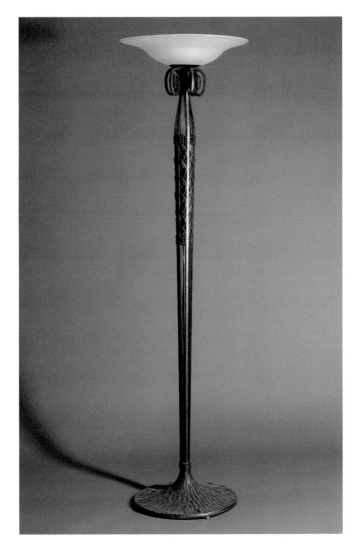

WROUGHT-IRON FLOOR LAMP (C. 1925)
Daum and Katona
Courtesy of Christie's Images

During the transition from gas to electric lighting, designers had to broach a number of new problems; the most pressing of these concerned the concealment of the electric wiring. One of the most common solutions was to feed it through a hollow stand, as in the pictured example. Normally, stands of this kind featured a minimum of decoration, but here there is a narrative theme. The shaft takes the form of a stylized Tree of Knowledge, and the serpent coils its way up the tree towards the source of the light.

The wrought-iron base is by Katona and the etched lampshade was made by the Daum brothers, Auguste (1853–1909) and Antonin (1864–1930) of Nancy. They ran a flourishing glass factory and also marketed a wide range of their own goods, which consisted mainly of vases and bowls. In addition, they worked in collaboration with other designers to produce mixed-media objects. Their most enduring partnership was with Edgar Brandt (1880–1960), the leading wrought-iron specialist. Together, they produced a variety of chandeliers and standard lamps. One, in particular, was very similar to this design, the difference being that Brandt managed to dispense with the tree. Instead, it was the snake's body that formed the shaft, holding up the lampshade as if it were a tempting bowl of fruit.

A SELECTION OF TABLE LAMPS WITH A VASE (1920s)
Desny and Jacques Le Chevalier
Courtesy of Christie's Images

This striking array of table lights illustrates the extraordinary variety of devices that were available in the 1920s, as well as the sheer inventiveness of some Modernist designs. It is interesting to note that the taste for severe geometric abstraction, heavily influenced by Cubism, did not detract from the practicality of the objects. The small circular lamp (bottom left) and the larger one on the right were both designed by Jacques Le Chevalier and produced by DIM (Décoration Intérieure Moderne). The latter was run by René Joubert, architect and cabinet-maker, and Georges Mouveau.

The remaining items, including the square metal vase in the front, were made by the firm of Desny. This short-lived concern operated for only a few years (1927–33) and consisted of just two men, Desnat and Nauny. Little is known about them, apart from the fact that they met while working for a circus. They sometimes designed complete decorative schemes, but generally specialized in small, geometric lights, which they described as *bibelots lumineux* ("luminous knick-knacks"). The small lamp at the back was particularly popular, and a similar model was marketed by Jean Perzel. The side flaps could be adjusted, making this the Cubist equivalent of an angle-poise lamp.

JADE CLOCK (C. 1927)
Cartier
Courtesy of Christie's Images

Few designers exploited the eclectic nature of Art Deco taste more fully than Cartier. In both his jewelry and his clocks, he combined geometric features with exotic, ornamental motifs from all over the world: Indian, Islamic, Oriental, and Egyptian elements all found their way into his work.

In this instance, the inspiration came from the Orient. The shape of the frame, the use of green jade, and the stylized animal design on the clock face all derive from the Far East, while the casing of the timepiece—most notably its stepped, geometric corners and the bold, angular numerals—is in a Western, Modernist vein.

Cartier was always particularly keen to draw attention to the surface of the clock face. He is credited with the invention of the "Mystery Clock", a novelty item that came onto the market in 1913. Through the use of a clever optical device, it appeared that the clock was operating without any mechanical works. Cartier is also said to have invented the wristwatch. In 1904, he designed one for his friend, a Brazilian aviator named Alberto Santos-Dumont (1873–1932), so that he would be able to tell the time without having to leave the controls of his plane.

PAINTED MANTEL CLOCK (C. 1928)
Sir Edwin Lutyens (1869–1944)
Courtesy of Christie's Images

Sir Edwin Lutyens is celebrated for his work as an architect, although he was also known to design furniture and smaller items as part of his larger commissions. This handsome clock, however, appears to have been created for private reasons, as a wedding present for one of his colleagues. It has a winding key in the shape of a pansy, which is stored in the miniature urn at the top. The clock's most unusual features, though, are the adjustable hands, which change length as they move round the oval dial.

Lutyens gave the clock to Sir Hubert Worthington when he married in 1928. The groom had worked briefly as Lutyens's assistant in 1912–13, before joining the family firm of Thomas Worthington and Sons. Despite the brevity of this working association, the pair had remained friends, and Lutyens was anxious to present the young man with a distinctive gift. Only three other copies are known to have been made. Two of these remained in Lutyens's family, while the third was given to the Vicereine of India. Worthington is best known for his restoration of Manchester Cathedral and the Radcliffe Camera in Oxford, while Lutyens's creations include Castle Drogo, Liverpool Cathedral, and the Cenotaph in Whitehall.

BRONZE MANTEL CLOCK (1925)
Louis Süe (1875–1968) and André Mare (1887–1932)

Courtesy of Christie's Images

Louis Süe trained in Paris as a painter, where he made contact with Paul Poiret. In 1911, the latter opened an influential design school, the Atelier Martine, and drawing his inspiration from this, Süe founded the Atelier Français in the following year. There, he designed a range of furniture, ceramics, and textiles.

Like Süe, André Mare began his career as a painter, creating a major impact at the 1912 Salon d'Automne with his *Maison Cubiste*. He made contact with Süe at around this time and, after the war, they formed a partnership, the Compagnie des Arts Français. For the next few years, the pair were at the forefront of Art Deco design, winning particular acclaim for their pavilion at the 1925 Paris Exhibition, which boasted the rather grand title of the *Musée de l'Art Contemporain*.

In common with other French designers, Süe and Mare were unimpressed by the functional angularity that Modernism had spawned. Instead, they decided that their products should evoke the more sumptuous designs of the Louis XV and Louis Philippe eras. This clock, designed for the firm by Pierre Poisson, is a typical example. Its ornate decoration recalls 18th-century models, while certain other features—the sunburst on the dial, the arrow-hands, the bold numerals—place it firmly in the Art Deco era.

A SELECTION OF CLOCKS AND A BUST (1920s)

Courtesy of Christie's Images

The brashness and vitality of Art Deco design are often most apparent in cheaper, mass-produced objects. The pictured items give some idea of the enormous choice that was available. The most conventional clocks are on the back (upper) row. On the left, there is a shagreen table clock with an ivory dial and, beside it, an English clock made out of chrome and shagreen.

The most overtly Art Deco item is the clock in the middle row. It was produced in France, and is made out of ivory and leather. Its octagonal shape is typical of the period, as is the geometric deployment of the numerals. In common with many Art Deco timepieces, the attention-grabbing nature of the design took precedence over the mundane business of actually telling the time.

The bottom left-hand item is a Hatot table clock, made out of chrome and glass. The stepped base and the oversized numerals are very much of their day. The right-hand piece is a Jaeger Le Coultre "Mystery Clock", a modest variant of the novelty format that had been invented by Cartier. The bronze bust in the center is by Somme. It features a woman dressed in the exotic style of costume that had been popularized by Chiparus and Preiss.

EUROPA AND THE BULL (C. 1925)
René Buthaud (1886–1986)
Courtesy of Christie's Images

René Buthaud was a versatile designer, known mainly for his ceramics and his graphic art. He came from Bordeaux, where he trained initially as a painter, but soon turned to ceramics, winning both the Prix Roux and the Prix Chenavard. The latter, named after Aimé Chenavard (1798–1838), a former adviser to the Sèvres factory, was particularly prestigious. Buthaud himself later held a similar position, when he was appointed director (1923–26) of the Primavera works at Tours. Its wares were marketed at the Printemps store in Paris and, by the mid-1920s, they were in the forefront of Art Deco design.

Buthaud's ceramic decoration betrays his origins as a painter. Much of his work features languorous, neoclassical nudes, provoking the suggestion that he was influenced by Jean Dupas, another native of Bordeaux, although similar images had already been popularized by Picasso and Matisse. Buthaud's nudes were confined mainly to his ceramics, but he also reproduced them on posters and prints. In this instance, the theme is a familiar story from Greek mythology. Zeus fell in love with Europa, the beautiful daughter of the king of Tyre. Assuming the shape of a bull, Zeus approached her as she was walking along the seashore and carried her off across the waves. Buthaud's maiden does not display the sense of alarm normally associated with this scene; her stylized hair is very characteristic of Art Deco design.

THREE VASES (1932)
René Lalique (1860–1945)
Courtesy of Christie's Images

René Lalique began his career as a trainee goldsmith, before setting up his own business. However, it was not until 1900 and the Paris Exhibition that he achieved international renown, securing his reputation as a major exponent of Art Nouveau. His interest in glass developed after 1906, when he was commissioned to design scent bottles for François Coty. At the 1925 Exhibition, Lalique had an entire pavilion devoted to his work, and also produced luxury goods for the Sèvres display.

The three items in this illustration, produced towards the end of his life, demonstrate the remarkable versatility of Lalique's designs. On the left, his *Ceylan* vase features four pairs of budgerigars in opalescent glass. Their long tail-feathers made this pattern particularly suitable for cylindrical designs. In the center, the *Bacchantes* pattern, with its energetic band of dancers, is the most overtly Art Deco of the trio. A version of the vase was featured at the 1925 Paris Exhibition. On the right, the bulbous green vase is decorated with an older *Gui* ("mistletoe") design. Lalique had been using this for some time, and it carries echoes of his earlier Art Nouveau style. The *Gui* pattern was employed on a variety of bowls and boxes; it was also used on the invitation-medallion for Lalique's 1912 exhibition.

Le Jour et la Nuit (Day and Night) (c. 1925)
René Lalique (1860–1945)
Courtesy of Christie's Images

This is the costliest and most elaborate of the many clocks Lalique produced for the luxury market; it retailed at the staggering price of 3500 francs. Set on a trapezoidal bronze base, the item was available in three different colors: blue, red-amber, and smoked purple.

Day and Night are symbolized by two nude figures. The lighter torso of the man represents the hours of daylight, while the shadowy figure of the woman, with one arm covering her eyes, indicates night. This contrast was heightened by the use of different production techniques: the man is intaglio-moulded, whilst his companion is moulded in relief.

Lalique may have had classical deities in mind when devising the figures for this piece. Apollo, the god who produced daylight by driving his sun-chariot across the sky, may have inspired the man, while Nyx, a goddess of the night, may have inspired his representation of the woman. It is equally possible, though, that he may simply have visualized the couple as a pair of unrequited lovers. Their bodies stretch and strain, forming two graceful arcs. Their feet overlap and their hands almost touch but, like day and night, they can never truly embrace.

HIRONDELLES (SWALLOWS) WALL-LIGHT (C. 1925)
René Lalique (1860–1945)
Courtesy of Christie's Images

Designers took a little while to adjust to the advent of electric lighting. With gas, the main focus of decoration had been on the lamp, but electricity offered much greater scope for ornamental glass. Through the addition of enameling or etching, light could be diffused in a variety of ways. Indirect lighting also became fashionable for the first time, as designers tried to soften the impact of electric light by reflecting it off walls or ceilings.

Lalique's first serious venture into the manufacture of light fittings began in the 1920s, at his Wingen factory. There, he designed an impressive range of products, including chandeliers, wall-lights, hanging lamps, and even illuminated statuettes. This particular example displays a typical Art Deco compromise between form and function. The shape of the fitting is simplicity itself, but the artist in Lalique could not resist the temptation to add moulded decoration. The *Hirondelles* pattern, showing a group of swallows in flight, was one of his favorites and he adapted it for use on a number of different objects. Among other places, it can be seen on vases, clocks, picture frames, cigarette boxes, and, most remarkable of all, car mascots.

SUZANNE (C. 1922)
René Lalique (1860–1945)
Courtesy of Christie's Images

Lalique's glass figurines are among the most famous of his Art Deco creations. He began producing statuettes of this kind in the early 1900s, initially using the *cire-perdue* ("lost wax") method. This proved too costly for commercial manufacture, however, and in the 1920s he switched to moulded figures. His most celebrated designs in this field were for a pair of female nudes, *Suzanne* and *Thaïs*. Both of these show young women emerging from the bath, holding up voluminous folds of drapery. The figure of *Suzanne* is thought to have been inspired by the Biblical story of Susanna and the Elders, although it is worth noting that Lalique's daughter was also called Suzanne.

The two statuettes were designed in 1922 and were manufactured until the mid-1930s. Approximately nine inches tall, they were intended for display on illuminated stands. A number of different formats were available—namely frosted, opalescent, or colored glass. The opalescent variety (pictured) was particularly attractive when lit from below. The earliest stands were made of bronze, decorated with peacocks and swirling bands of flowers, but for reasons of economy these were replaced with plain, rectangular pedestals.

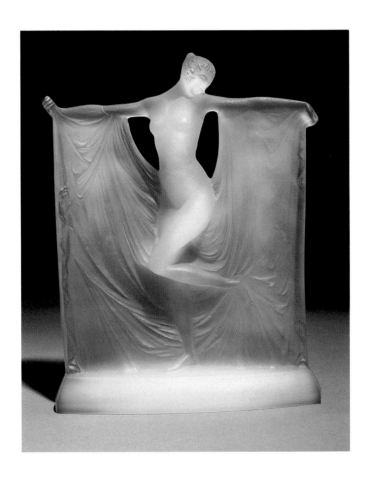

THE ARISTOCRATS (1920s)
Professor Otto Poertzel (1876–)
Courtesy of Christie's Images

This is one of the best known examples of Art Deco sculpture. If it were not for the medieval outfit, it might easily have been representative of a Hollywood starlet arriving at a premiere with a pair of borzois. Certainly, it conjures up the archetypal woman of the period—tall, slender, and extremely chic. The popularity of the sculpture is confirmed by the fact that Ferdinand Preiss (1882–1943) marketed an almost identical figure (the distinction is the position of the two dogs). They are so similar that at one stage it was argued that Poertzel was a pseudonym for Preiss. In fact, very little is known about this sculptor, including whether or not he was a genuine professor. He is thought to have been born in Scheiben, Germany, in 1876 and to have worked mainly in Coburg. He is believed to have specialized in sculpting nightclub dancers and circus performers.

Statuettes of this kind are frequently referred to as "chryselephantine." Technically, this term referred only to figures made out of ivory and gold, and was usually applied to carvings produced in ancient Greece. By the 19th century, however, it was common to use the term to describe any multimedia carving made of ivory and another high-quality material, such as bronze, marble, or onyx.

BUTTERFLY DANCERS (1920s)
Professor Otto Poertzel (1876–)
Courtesy of Christie's Images

This was one of the best-selling examples of Art Deco carving. In common with *The Aristocrats*, almost identical versions were produced by both Preiss and Poertzel (Preiss's version was marketed as *The Twins*). This raises the question of whether Poertzel was working for Preiss's firm or whether the two men were in competition. Butterfly dancers were a popular theme for sculptors of this period. The name derives from the way that the girls' flowing skirts are attached to their hands, giving them a superficial resemblance to wings, when the dance is in progress.

The taste for carvings of this kind had originated in Belgium at the end of the previous century, stimulated by a huge glut of ivory imports from the Belgian Congo. As a result, registered artists were given the material free of charge and further encouragement was offered, in the form of lucrative state commissions. Through such measures, the genre became extremely popular for a time, especially with the artists of the Symbolist movement.

By the time of the First World War, however, ivory carvings seemed outdated; with the introduction of cheaper, modern methods for casting bronze and other metals, it became financially viable to aim these products at the popular market. It was here that they found their niche during the Art Deco years.

A SELECTION OF BRONZE AND IVORY DANCERS (1920s)

Courtesy of Christie's Images

Despite their similarity, these energetic dancers were designed by a number of competing sculptors, which is an indication of the strength of the market at the time. From the left, they consist of a pair of *Bacchantes* carved by G. Omerth and set on marble bases; a *Dancer* by Henri Fugère; a *Corinthian Dancer* by Claire Colinet; and a restrained depiction of *Aphrodite* by Ferdinand Preiss.

The best-known artists in this group were Colinet and Preiss. Claire Colinet hailed from Belgium, where she studied sculpture under Jef Lambeaux. Moving to Paris, she exhibited regularly at both the Salon des Indépendants and the Salon des Artistes Français. Her style was closest to that of Chiparus, although in her work there was more emphasis on movement than mystery. Ferdinand Preiss was the most prolific artist in this field. A German by birth, he began his career in Milan, before returning to Berlin to set up a business with his friend, Arthur Kassler. Preiss's naturalistic style was extremely popular, especially in England where, in view of postwar, anti-German sentiments, he described himself as an Austrian. Many of his female figures can be readily identified as contemporary stars from the music-hall or the movie theater.

A SELECTION OF BRONZE AND IVORY FIGURINES (1920s)
Ferdinand Preiss (1882–1943)
Courtesy of Christie's Images

Ferdinand Preiss was the most entrepreneurial of the Art Deco sculptors. In 1906, with Arthur Kassler, he set up a private company, Preiss-Kassler, to market their wares. He specialized above all in dancers, producing them in series that were aimed specifically at collectors. These usually focused on different dances, such as the Charleston or the more exotic Snake Dance, or on a variety of costumes. Here, the *Cabaret Girl* (third from left) represents a nightclub dancer, while the *Spanish Dancer* (extreme left) comes from a series depicting national costumes. It was not executed by Preiss himself, but by Paul Philippe, one of a team of artists who produced work for Preiss-Kassler.

The remaining figures are *Powderpuff* (right) and *Ecstasy* (second from left). The former typically represents a contemporary woman, a very popular subject in the 1920s. The woman's mirror, shoes, and headgear provide an interesting record of fashions of the time, although the skimpy dress would have been worn only by a chorus girl as a stage costume. At first glance, *Ecstasy* appears to be a very traditional nude, which could have been produced at almost any other artistic period. In fact, this particular subject was extremely common with Art Deco artists, although it is better known in other media. Its most popular use was as a car mascot, typified by Rolls-Royce's *Spirit of Ecstasy*.

A Selection of Bronze and Ivory Figurines
Ferdinand Preiss (1882–1943)
Courtesy of Christie's Images

This fine array of figurines demonstrates the extraordinary versatility of Ferdinand Preiss. From the left, the top row consists of a *Torch Dancer*; a tiny *Pierrette*; *Thoughts*, an onyx and marble mantel clock; and a *Moth Girl*. Beneath this, the second row consists of a *Grecian with Torch*; the *Oriental Waiter* who was sometimes described as a *Turkish Boy*; *Ecstasy*, *Victorian Lady*; and the *Golfer*.

Preiss widened his range by introducing tiny variations in the accessories and then marketing the marginally different pieces as distinct works. The *Moth Girl*, for example, was also available as the *Champagne Dancer*: yet the two figures were identical, apart from the fact that the latter woman was holding a glass, rather than a moth, in her left hand. Similarly, Preiss attempted to increase the saleability of his goods by making them more functional. Thus, ivory bathers became an ornamental feature on some clocks, and the popular *Ecstasy* figure was marketed with a variety of dishes and ashtrays.

The *Golfer* is an example of Preiss's sporting themes, which were also much in demand at the time. This formed part of the so-called Olympic series, which included individual sports and physical exercises. The series was produced as a reaction to public interest in the Olympic Games, which were staged for the first time in 1896. Sadly these sporting figurines went out of fashion, owing to the Nazi preoccupation with staging grandiose public displays of physical exercises at their rallies.

LES AMIS DE TOUJOURS (FRIENDS FOREVER) (1920S)
Dimitri Chiparus
Courtesy of Christie's Images

Dimitri (or Demêtre) Chiparus was probably the most talented of the many Art Deco sculptors who worked in ivory. He was born in Romania, but worked mainly in Paris, where he received an Honourable Mention at the Salon des Artistes Français in 1914; he continued to exhibit there until 1928. Chiparus's figurines were noted for the jewel-like treatment of their costume and their elaborate bases. In this instance, the woman is standing on a relatively simple brown onyx pedestal, but some examples had geometrical bases adorned with secondary figures in relief.

By and large, Art Deco figurines were aimed at the popular market, but Chiparus's work is more akin to the output of the previous generation of ivory workers, when artists such as Fernand Khnopff (1858–1921) and Sir Alfred Gilbert (1854–1934) produced moody, symbolic pieces for connoisseurs. This particular piece displays some very modern features (the close-fitting cap, the pendant earrings, the elegant borzois), but it also has an enigmatic, medieval air. Chiparus specialized principally in dancers. These ranged from elegant, balletic figures, inspired by the dancers in the Ballets Russes, to more flamboyant images, based on performers from Parisian nightclubs. He also produced mysterious, symbolic figures, such as *Obéissance* and *La Mystérieuse*.

A Selection of Bronze and Ivory Figurines (1920s)

Courtesy of Christie's Images

This is an assortment of chryselephantine figures by some of the lesser-known sculptors of the Art Deco period, giving an idea of the very wide range of themes and styles that were on the market. From the right, they are a *Minstrel* by Roland Paris; *The Golden Wedding* by A. Becquerel; a *Dancing Girl* by Samuel Lipchytz; *The Riding Crop* by Bruno Zach; and a female nude by Toni Weinkopf.

The best-known artist in this group was Zach, an Austrian sculptor who specialized in erotic themes. Most of his work consists of scantily-clad young girls, smoking cigarettes, and posing provocatively. His figures occasionally have sado-masochistic overtones, although the subject is always treated with humor. Even at a cursory glance, it is clear that dancers provided the most popular subject matter for sculptors of this period. They were usually in modern dress or in exotic costumes inspired by the Ballets Russes, but they could also be found in the traditional Pierrot and Columbine outfits, or in imaginary medieval dress. The *Golden Wedding* statuette illustrates the changing nature of the ivory market. A generation earlier, figures such as this had been aimed squarely at the art connoisseur; by the 1920s, however, they had become acceptable presents for occasions such as anniversaries, weddings, or retirement.

BOOK COVER (1927)
Jean Dunand (1887–1942)
Courtesy of Christie's Images

With the advent of Art Deco designs, the craft of bookbinding received a much-needed boost. In France, most books were still published with flimsy covers, and even collector's editions were conservatively bound in leather. Art Deco bindings introduced two significant innovations. Some covers featured the bold, geometric designs that can be found on many typical artefacts of the period, while other designers preferred to experiment with unusual materials. Dunand, for example, decorated his covers with tiny plaques made out of lacquer, *coquille d'oeuf* (crushed eggshell), or inlaid marquetry. Similarly, some of his fellow designers incorporated panels of ivory, bronze, or precious stones into their work. In the pictured example, Dunand has executed a small lacquerware medallion, based on a drawing by François-Louis Schmied (1873–1941). The exotic nature of this plaque was highly appropriate for the book, an oriental romance entitled *Histoire charmante de l'Adolescente Sucre d'Amour* ("A Charming Tale of the Sweetest Little Girl").

Dunand worked initially in the Art Nouveau style before embracing Art Deco. After becoming a specialist in lacquerware, he applied it to screens, furniture, and interiors, as well as book covers. At the 1925 Exhibition, he had stunned spectators with a black lacquer smoking room designed for the French Embassy. Later he won commissions from three of the largest liners: the *Ile de France* (1928), the *Atlantique* (1931), and the *Normandie* (1935).

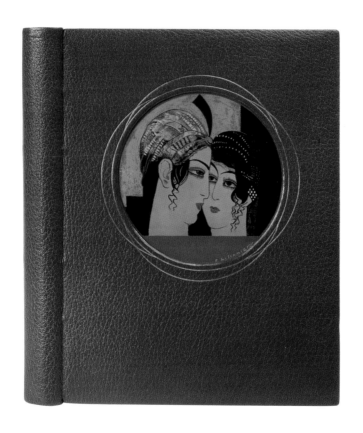

OUVERT LA NUIT (1924)
Pierre Legrain (1887–1929)

Courtesy of Christie's Images

Pierre Legrain is widely regarded as the most innovative of the Art Deco bookbinders. This is all the more remarkable because he came to the craft through a chapter of accidents. In 1904, he entered the Ecole des Arts Appliqués, but was forced to abandon his course after his father's business collapsed. Legrain helped support his family by selling cartoons and, through these, he gained employment from the satirist Paul Iribe (Iribarnegaray— 1883–1935). His career was disrupted for a second time, however, when Iribe emigrated to the US and the war intervened. Desperate for work, Legrain agreed to design modern covers for Jacques Doucet's (1853–1929) sizable book collection, even though he had no experience in this area of design. In spite of this, the project proved a great success and Legrain established his own bindery in 1923.

The pictured example is one of Legrain's finest covers. It was commissioned for Paul Morand's *Ouvert La Nuit* ("Open at Night"), published in a limited edition of 320 copies. With just a few geometric shapes and some imaginative use of calligraphy, the designer manages to conjure up the excitement of city nightlife. The nocturnal background is studded with bright, golden circles, which represent electric lighting— enlarged for effect, as in O'Keeffe's *Moon in New York*—while the eye-catching title resembles the kind of sign that might be found outside a bar or nightclub.

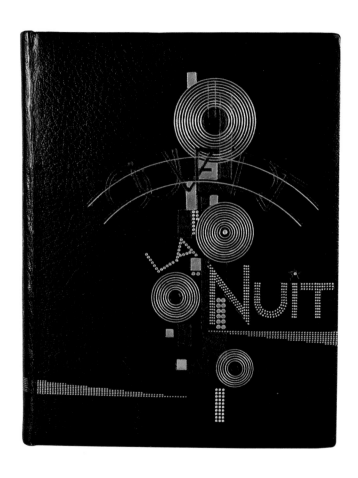

LA CRÉATION (THE CREATION) (1928)
François-Louis Schmied (1873–1941)
Courtesy of Christie's Images

This is a de luxe edition of *The Creation*, consisting of the first three books of *Genesis*, together with a Biblical genealogy. It was produced by Joseph-Charles Mardus and was issued in a limited edition of 175 copies. The decoration of the binding and the woodcut illustrations accompanying the text were designed by François-Louis Schmied. The cosmic theme of the book was ideally suited to Art Deco styles of decoration. The swirling act of creation and the emission of blinding shafts of light were easy to render in geometric terms, and the image as a whole bears a notable similarity to the sunburst, the most characteristic of all Art Deco motifs.

Schmied was a Swiss graphic artist and printer. He studied at the Ecole des Arts Industriels in Geneva, where one of his fellow students was Jean Dunand. They would later work together on a number of book projects. As an illustrator, Schmied's most notable collaboration was with Paul Jouve (1889–1973), on an edition of *The Jungle Book*. During the First World War, Schmied enlisted with the Foreign Legion and lost an eye during the hostilities. This did not prevent him from working, however, and in the 1920s he operated in most areas of book production—as a publisher, printer, illustrator, and typographer. Despite initial success, his career declined during the Depression and he died a virtual pauper.

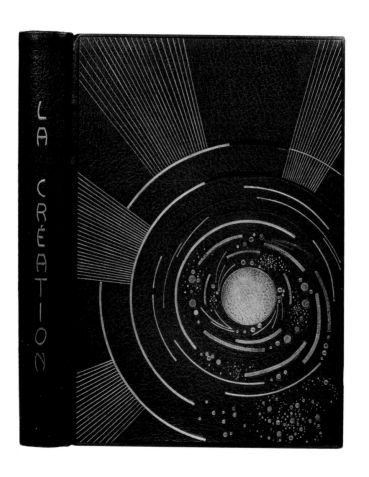

AUTHOR BIOGRAPHIES AND ACKNOWLEDGMENTS

Iain Zaczek comes from Dundee in Scotland. He was educated at Wadham College, Oxford, and the Courtauld Institute of Art. Over recent years, he has written widely on artistic and Celtic themes. His books include *Impressionist Interiors*, *The Art of Illuminated Manuscripts*, *The Book of Kells*, *The Art of the Icon*, and *Essential Morris*.

Dr Mike O'Mahoney studied History of Art at the Courtauld Institute of Art, where he completed his doctoral thesis on Official Art in the Soviet Union between the Wars. He has taught at the Courtauld Institute, Winchester School of Art, and Reading University, and has lectured at the Tate Gallery and the Victoria and Albert Museum in London.

While every endeavor has been made to ensure the accuracy of the reproduction of the images in this book, we would be grateful to receive any comments or suggestions for inclusion in future reprints.

With thanks to Christie's Images and the Architectural Association for assistance with sourcing the pictures for this book. Grateful thanks to Helen Courtney for her design input, Bridget Tily for picture research, and Sasha Heseltine for editorial assistance.